VOLUME

OLD TESTAM

THE NEW COLLEGEVILLE BIBLE COMMENTARY

PROVERBS

Katherine M. Hayes

SERIES EDITOR

Daniel Durken, O.S.B.

LITURGICAL PRESS

Collegeville, Minnesota

www.litpress.org

Nihil Obstat: Reverend Robert Harren, *Censor deputatus.*
Imprimatur: ✢ Most Reverend John F. Kinney, J.C.D., D.D., Bishop of Saint Cloud, Minnesota. April 15, 2013.

Design by Ann Blattner.

Cover illustration: Detail of *Seven Pillars of Wisdom* by Donald Jackson. © 2007 *The Saint John's Bible*, Order of Saint Benedict, Collegeville, Minnesota. Used with permission. All rights reserved.

Photos: pages 19, 25, 38, 54, 70, 86, and 104, Thinkstock Photos.

1   2   3   4   5   6   7   8   9

Library of Congress Cataloging-in-Publication Data

Hayes, Katherine Murphey.
  Proverbs / Katherine M. Hayes ; series editor, Daniel Durken, O.S.B.
      pages   cm. — (New Collegeville Bible commentary. Old Testament ; volume 18)
  Includes index.
  ISBN 978-0-8146-2852-2
  1. Bible. O.T. Proverbs—Commentaries.   I. Durken, Daniel.   II. Title.

  BS1465.53.H39   2012
  223'.7077—dc23   2012034886

CONTENTS

ABBREVIATIONS

Books of the Bible

Acts—Acts of the Apostles
Amos—Amos
Bar—Baruch
1 Chr—1 Chronicles
2 Chr—2 Chronicles
Col—Colossians
1 Cor—1 Corinthians
2 Cor—2 Corinthians
Dan—Daniel
Deut—Deuteronomy
Eccl (or Qoh)—Ecclesiastes
Eph—Ephesians
Esth—Esther
Exod—Exodus
Ezek—Ezekiel
Ezra—Ezra
Gal—Galatians
Gen—Genesis
Hab—Habakkuk
Hag—Haggai
Heb—Hebrews
Hos—Hosea
Isa—Isaiah
Jas—James
Jdt—Judith
Jer—Jeremiah
Job—Job
Joel—Joel
John—John
1 John—1 John
2 John—2 John
3 John—3 John
Jonah—Jonah
Josh—Joshua
Jude—Jude
Judg—Judges
1 Kgs—1 Kings

2 Kgs—2 Kings
Lam—Lamentations
Lev—Leviticus
Luke—Luke
1 Macc—1 Maccabees
2 Macc—2 Maccabees
Mal—Malachi
Mark—Mark
Matt—Matthew
Mic—Micah
Nah—Nahum
Neh—Nehemiah
Num—Numbers
Obad—Obadiah
1 Pet—1 Peter
2 Pet—2 Peter
Phil—Philippians
Phlm—Philemon
Prov—Proverbs
Ps(s)—Psalms
Rev—Revelation
Rom—Romans
Ruth—Ruth
1 Sam—1 Samuel
2 Sam—2 Samuel
Sir—Sirach
Song—Song of Songs
1 Thess—1 Thessalonians
2 Thess—2 Thessalonians
1 Tim—1 Timothy
2 Tim—2 Timothy
Titus—Titus
Tob—Tobit
Wis—Wisdom
Zech—Zechariah
Zeph—Zephaniah

The Book of Proverbs

The Purpose and Ethos of Proverbs

In some ways the English word "proverb" is misleading as a title for this book because it gives the impression of folksy, simplistic advice that is familiar to the point of boredom. In fact the Hebrew word behind "proverb" is better translated as "memorable saying." This book resembles a collection of the wit and wisdom of Shakespeare or an anthology of Japanese haiku. The observations of Proverbs are carefully crafted: poetic, subtle, multifaceted, playful or ironic, and profound. Their wit prompts the reader to think more clearly about the various dimensions of human existence.

The intent of Proverbs, as stated in the prologue (1:1-7), is that this sort of thinking will lead to insight and understanding about the world that can inform the way one lives. Delightful as they are to read and ponder, the sayings of this book are devised to teach, furthering the growth in character we call wisdom and thus enhancing the quality of one's life.

The wisdom in which Proverbs aims to instruct its readers is comprehensive. It ranges from the practical to the psychological to the ethical. It includes management of one's own life, relations with others, and, in places, the governance of a nation. It is pervaded with reminders about the activity and presence of God in human life, and it is founded in awareness, or fear, of the Lord (1:7; 9:10; 21:30).

In its central contrast between the ways of the just and the wicked, the wisdom of Proverbs reflects a communal ethos evident also in the biblical law codes and the prophetic literature. This is clear in sayings that point to practices like the bearing of false witness, adultery, mistreatment of parents, accepting bribes, falsification of weights and measures, exploitation or indifference to the poor, and ritual observance that is unaccompanied by human decency. Proverbs explores the implications of these practices from various angles. The sayings extend beyond these areas, however, to encompass many others: neighborly relations, marital relations, child rearing, speech and conversation, friendship, work, and human emotions and individuality. They touch on the whole quality of a person's life.

In their range the sayings reflect an understanding of the integral relationship between the life of the individual and the life of the social body. What each individual does or doesn't do affects the quality and character of the community. The community as a whole attains stability and thrives when its members prosper and know how to live peaceably with each other. At the same time, the way an individual's life develops is influenced by the community's response to that person's decisions and actions. If these habitually cause conflict and trouble, if they are abusive or simply misguided and inept, the person will eventually face opposition or social stigma (shame). Hence the significance of honor and a good name, which bring the trust and good will that are vital if an individual is to flourish and that can be passed on to children. A good name is of more value than riches (Prov 22:1).

Overall, Proverbs can be seen as guiding members of the community, especially the young, in how to get on and how to get along in life. In some instances the observations and counsels of this book are culturally limited, but for the most part they are formulated in language that speaks universally of the human condition.

The Structure of the Book of Proverbs

The title "The Proverbs of Solomon" (Prov 1:1) applies to the entire book, yet the book encompasses collections of sayings clearly attributed to other figures. Proverbs is in fact a composite of various writings. Nine sections are usually distinguished.

1:1-7	Prologue
1:8–9:18	Introduction
10:1–22:16	The Proverbs of Solomon
22:17–24:22	The Sayings of the Wise
24:23-34	Other Sayings of the Wise
25:1–29:27	Other Proverbs of Solomon
30:1-33	The Words of Agur
31:1-9	The Words of Lemuel
31:10-31	The Worthy Woman

The overall structure of the book consists of a central core of sayings and instructions (Prov 10–29) that is prefaced by a long introduction (Prov 1–9), and ends with concluding reflections and a poem (Prov 30–31). The introduction creates a broad framework of wisdom for the sayings, the concluding reflections echo this framework, and the final poem transforms all that has been said about wisdom into a human portrait.

The Authorship and Origins of Proverbs

The titles of the discrete collections within Proverbs suggest diverse origins. The notation in Proverbs 25:1 that other proverbs of Solomon were transmitted by the "servants of Hezekiah, king of Judah," who lived several centuries after Solomon, points to stages of compilation and editing over time. The claim of Solomonic authorship for the book in 1:1 places the entire work within the tradition associated with a wise and just king who "uttered three thousand proverbs" (1 Kgs 5:12). This claim is meaningful but does not tell the whole story.

Because the sayings of Proverbs elucidate fundamental human situations, they offer few clues to the particular contexts of their composition. The roles of both father and mother in teaching children are mentioned in the book, however, and some scholars propose that the sayings and instructions in their earliest forms were associated with the formation of character of the young in the home (23:22, 25; 29:15; 30:17; 31:1; cf. 1:8; 4:3; 6:20). That various proverbs speak of the role of the king or ruler suggests, further, a historical context under the monarchy (14:28; 16:10, 12-15; 20:8, 26, 28; 21:1; 29:4, 14), as does the reference to King Hezekiah in 25:1.

The literary quality of Proverbs makes it likely that colloquial sayings were not simply collected but also selected, refashioned, and composed by royal scribes: men trained in reading, writing, and composition and familiar with the language and literature of other cultures. Scribes were probably associated with the royal court before the exile (e.g., the "servants of Hezekiah"). To them may be attributed sayings that pertain to working closely with kings and rulers or holding positions of power (14:35; 22:11, 29; 23:1-8, 10-11; 24:21; 25:1-7, 15). The task of collecting and writing wise sayings, however, cannot be definitively traced or limited to the reign of Solomon in the 10th century B.C.

After the exile scribal activity may have been associated with both the temple and independent scribal schools. The introduction and conclusion to Proverbs (chs. 1–9 and 30–31) were probably added at a later stage of redaction, well into the postexilic period.

Some scholars propose that early written collections of sayings and instructions were read and copied in Israel, along with other forms of literature, in schools training young men as scribes (and possibly as potential leaders and officials as well). That scribal schools existed in Egypt and Mesopotamia is clear in texts preserved from these cultures. In a school setting the copying and reciting of proverbial material would have contributed to the moral and psychological development of students as well as to their literary skills. Schools in Israel may have ensured the preservation of the proverbs as part of a communal treasury of wisdom handed down within families over many generations.

Literary Forms in Proverbs

Wisdom is praised and taught in Proverbs in three major literary forms: (1) instructions, (2) wisdom poems, and (3) sayings. Following are examples of each type, (2) being an *excerpt* of a wisdom poem.

> (1) Hear, my son, and be wise,
>   and guide your heart in the right way.
> Do not join with wine bibbers,
>   nor with those who glut themselves on meat;
> For drunkards and gluttons come to poverty,
>   and lazing about clothes one in rags. (Prov 23:19-21)

> (2) Long life is in her right hand,
>   in her left are riches and honor;
> Her ways are pleasant ways,
>   and all her paths are peace;
> She is a tree of life to those who grasp her,
>   and those who hold her fast are happy. (Prov 3:16-18)

> (3) The naive believe everything,
>   but the shrewd watch their steps. (Prov 14:15)

Instructions deliver advice in imperative form, either positive (a command) or negative (an admonition). As in example 1 above, many begin with a direct address ("my son") and an appeal to listen ("hear," "guide your heart"). The directive itself ("do not join") is often followed by an explanation ("for drunkards and gluttons come to poverty"). The parental speeches in chapters 1–9 are a form of instruction, as are many of the "Sayings of the Wise" in 22:17–24:22 and "The Words of Lemuel" in 31:1-9. Instructions are to the point and press the reader to take a specified course of action. They rely on the personal tone and conviction of the speaker (often the parent) to persuade.

Wisdom poems praising or speaking of wisdom as a distinct quality, as in example 2 above, are found in chapters 1–9, interwoven with the parental speeches. In these poems wisdom is often personified as a woman ("Long life is in her right hand"), and this is matched by the embodiment of wisdom in the worthy woman who is the subject of the book's concluding poem (31:10-31). The lyric tone, archetypal imagery, and cosmic language of these poems awaken in the reader an attraction to wisdom as a way of life.

Sayings in Proverbs typically take the form of a one line, two-part, aphorism, as in example 3, but include some multi-verse units, such as the lists of phenomena known as "numerical sayings" in Proverbs 30. "Saying" is a translation of the Hebrew word *mashal*, which is used in the Old Testament to refer to a range of types of speech (see, e.g., 1 Sam 24:14; Ezek 17:1-10; Jer 24:9; Num 23:7-10). As noted above, the word is probably best understood as a "memorable utterance."

Sayings, in contrast to instructions, are for the most part not explicit directives. Rather, they provide miniature sketches of human behavior and attitude. Often they contrast different types of behavior, as in example 3 above, where the unthinking acceptance of the naive person is contrasted with the careful reckoning of the shrewd. Often the consequences of specified behaviors or attitudes are contrasted as well. In these ways the sayings provide "food for thought" for the reader.

All of Proverbs is poetic in form. The kind of figurative language that is characteristic of poetry—image, metaphor, word play, personification, irony—is densely clustered in these writings. In terms of poetic structure, all exhibit the characteristic feature of Hebrew poetry called *parallelism*. This means that they are composed in poetic lines that divide syntactically into two-part (occasionally three-part) lines, which complement and interact with each other. *Synonymous parallelism* occurs when half-lines echo each other in some way, as in example 1 above. *Antithetic parallelism* means that the half-lines contrast with each other, as in example 3. Finally, *synthetic parallelism* refers to instances in which the half-lines simply complete each other, as in the last line of example 2. The natural but often inexact pairing of the half-lines allows for many possible points of connection and contrast.

The Artistic and Didactic Mode of the Saying

Because the two-part saying dominates in Proverbs, it is helpful to consider briefly its mode of expression and teaching. First, these sayings represent a particularly compressed form of poetry. There is no room in them for elaboration or explanation, and thus the resonant quality of the poetic language is intensified. The images they raise are concrete, yet evoke multiple associations (see, e.g., the image of the shrewd person watching his or her steps in example 3 above). In this respect the proverbial sayings are not unlike the seventeen-syllable poetic form of the Japanese haiku.

Second, many of the sayings effect a comparison or contrast, which is heightened by the parallelism of the compound poetic line. Antithetic parallelism sharpens a contrast, as in example 3, but the sayings include many other types of comparison and contrast. The "better than" sayings compare two situations by declaring the one named in the first half-line to be better than the one named in the second (15:17, 16:8, 32; 17:1; 19:1; 27:5; 28:6). The "happy are" sayings compare by implication those pronounced happy with those who are not (14:21; 16:20; 20:7; 28:14; 29:18). The "abomination" sayings, which declare certain types of behavior as an abomination to God or to others, can be seen similarly (11:1; 15:8; 21:27; 28:9).

"Like" sayings spread a simile over two half-lines (10:26; 11:22; 25:11-14, 18-20; 26:1, 8-10; 27:19; 28:15). Other sayings accomplish this sort of comparison without using the word "like" (26:7, 14; 27:17-18, 20), and many others employ similes or metaphors in one half-line or the other (16:31; 17:8; 18:8; 20:1, 27; 21:1; 22:4; 25:4). In all these instances the sayings instruct by inviting the reader to ponder just how the things compared are related or different, better or worse. As thoughts reverberate in the mind, one's understanding is expanded.

Each saying, then, opens up associations, and each is intended to be read as a small poem. For the most part, there is no discernible principle of order in the sequence of sayings in Proverbs. This need not be problematic if each is contemplated on its own terms.

At the same time, the sayings have been gathered together into different collections and into one overarching collection, and it is natural to read them in relation to each other. Apparent contradictions in perspective should not surprise the reader (e.g., 10:10 and 11:12; 10:15 and 11:4, 28; 11:15 and 11:24-25; 26:4-5; 28:1 and 28:15). Most sayings reflect a particular insight that sheds light on an aspect of human experience. None intends to encompass all the complexities of a situation or to preclude other angles of vision.

Rather, it is left to the reader to weigh the different perspectives and to consider their appropriateness in different contexts. When, for example, is it helpful to confront or reprove (10:10) and when to keep silent (11:12)? When is wealth (or equity) to be valued for the stability it brings to life (10:15) and when is it overvalued (11:28)? The gathering of distinct sayings into a collection makes possible a second level of comparison in Proverbs. The comparison *between* sayings also furthers the reader's growth in wisdom.

This is as true for the resemblances between sayings as for the differences. There are a few instances where sayings are repeated word for word, or practically so (18:8 and 26:22; 19:5 and 19:9; 20:16 and 27:13; 21:9 and 25:24; 22:13 and 26:13). Many more express similar perspectives with distinctive language and imagery. The recurrent patterns help the reader build up in his or her mind an impression of the contours of wisdom as an approach to life.

The Nature and Limits of Wisdom in Proverbs

The wisdom of Proverbs is optimistic. Its basic premise is that life is made up of choices, and its basic tenet that the ability to make good choices can be learned. By attending to the inherited ethos represented by parental instruction and reflecting on the connections displayed in the sayings (especially the connections between behavior and outcome), the reader sees life's realities and choices more clearly. He or she learns to discern what is appropriate and of lasting value and gains competence in responding thoughtfully in all the moments that compose a life. The result is well-being beyond price. In the words of Proverbs 19:8, those who acquire the sensibility of wisdom (literally, "gain heart") love themselves, and those who actively maintain understanding find what is good in life. It is a good that tastes sweet to the soul and that instills hope:

> If you eat honey, my son, because it is good
> if pure honey is sweet to your taste;
> Such, you must know, is wisdom to your soul.
> If you find it, you will have a future,
> and your hope will not be cut off. (Prov 24:13-14)

The speeches and poems of chapters 1–9 further assert that if one trusts in the promise of wisdom (and in the parental figures who teach it) and opens oneself to learn, wisdom will inhabit the heart, directing one's actions and saving one from serious missteps and wrongdoing as if by intuition (2:1-22; 3:21-26). Wisdom is ultimately a habit of being that is greater than the sum of its parts. It is, in fact, a transcendent quality that comes from God (2:6; 8:22-31). Personifying wisdom as a woman, chapters 8 and 9 show her delight in human beings and her desire to become the intimate companion of all (8:17, 31; 9:1-6; cf. 7:4).

Fools are those who have not pursued or who reject this possibility of companionship and well-being. They range from the naïve or unthinking, to the obtuse who are set in their own ways, to the arrogant and perverse who dismiss any thought of change or improvement. Fools are headed for trouble because they have not accepted wisdom's promise of protection and presence.

The focus of Proverbs, then, is on what can be learned from the contemplation of traditional teachings and of wisdom itself as a transcendent power. The book is not primarily concerned with life situations that are unexpected, inexplicable, or seemingly unconnected to human choice. There are sayings in Proverbs that depict these sorts of situations. Some speak of the ultimate role of God, rather than of human wisdom, in the unfolding of human experience. For example:

> The human heart plans the way,
> > but the LORD directs the steps (16:9).

Or:

> Our steps are from the LORD;
> > how, then, can mortals understand their way? (20:24).

Other sayings present certain existential or social realities as givens, such as anxiety and sadness (13:12; 14:10, 13), the shunning or oppression of the poor (13:23; 14:20; 18:23; 19:7; 28:3), the injustice of rulers (28:15-16; 29:4), and the allure of wrongdoing (17:8, 18:8) or foolishness (26:11). Such observations seem to foster a sense of realistic acceptance more than of proactive choice. Yet in light of the overall teaching mode of Proverbs, sayings like these can be seen as challenging the reader to work out their implications for living wisely. This challenge is taken up in depth in the books of Job and Ecclesiastes.

Gender in Proverbs

When the vantage point of gender is either specified or implied in Proverbs, it is almost entirely male. The speaker in the ten parental speeches in chapters 1–9, which serve as a literary frame for the book, is a father who addresses his son. It is true that the father links his teaching with that of the mother in 1:8 and 6:20, and we might presume that he serves as the spokesperson for a tradition of wisdom that is passed down from the older generation—mother and father alike—to the younger. But the mother's wisdom is generally articulated by her husband. It is the son, moreover, who is singled out as the novice in wisdom. He is repeatedly, and at length, warned against committing adultery with another man's wife (2:16-19; 5:1-23; 6:20-35; 7:1-27). The perspective given on this particular form of foolishness is clearly male.

The sayings in chapters 10–29 refer to the role of both father and mother in the formation of the young (10:1; 15:20; 23:22; 29:15; 30:17). "The Words of Lemuel" in 31:1-9, further, are identified as the teaching of Lemuel's mother (31:1), thus balancing at the end of the book the parental speeches delivered by the father at the beginning. Yet on the whole, when gender features in a saying or instruction in the body of the book, the focus is, again, on the male (11:16; 15:25; 23:25b; 29:15; and 30:23 could be considered exceptions). This is clear in sayings that speak of finding a spouse (11:22; 12:4; 18:22; 19:14), the experience of marriage (21:9, 19; 25:24; 27:15-16), and the dangers of adultery (22:14; 23:27-28; 30:20). The naming of King Lemuel as the recipient of his mother's teaching provides another example.

This imbalance in perspective may be related to the literary adaptation of traditional wisdom by scribal circles and to the use of such adaptations in scribal schools. The profession of scribe was limited to men, and the schools trained only boys and young men. As noted above, however, many scholars believe that the basic formation in character that underlies the sayings was centered in the home and naturally included children of both sexes.

The majority of the sayings and instructions in Proverbs make no explicit reference to gender and can be read from the viewpoint of both men and women. The personification of wisdom as a woman and potential companion in the introduction of the book (chs. 1–9) and the manifestation of wisdom in the worthy woman in the conclusion to the book (31:10-31) may have been intended to stir the imaginations of men. At the same time they cannot help but do the same for the women who, as seekers of wisdom, read Proverbs today.

Proverbs Today and Tomorrow

Proverbs represents the ongoing search for a way of being in the world that is life-giving and fruitful. It illuminates the varied realities and circumstances of human experience, while mindful of the presence and activity of God. John Henry Cardinal Newman's affirmation of the pursuit of knowledge in his *The Idea of a University* reflects this kind of conscious integration:

> We attain to heaven by using this world well, though it is to pass away; we perfect our nature, not by undoing it, but by adding to it what is more than nature and directing it towards aims higher than its own.

In Proverbs, wisdom is a search that each person must undertake for him or herself. Wisdom is above all an endeavor. The sayings, instructions, and poems of Proverbs invite us to become students or disciples of wisdom, striving continually to comprehend what it means to be wise in our own time and place and as our circumstances change. In opening up this possibility for sincere seekers, wisdom's value is unchanging: "she is a tree of life to those who grasp her" (Prov 3:18).

The Book of Proverbs

I. Title and Introduction

Purpose of the Proverbs of Solomon

1 [1]The proverbs of Solomon, the son
    of David,
    king of Israel:
[2]That people may know wisdom
    and discipline,
    may understand intelligent
    sayings;
[3]May receive instruction in wise
    conduct,
    in what is right, just and fair;
[4]That resourcefulness may be im-
    parted to the naive,
    knowledge and discretion to the
    young.
[5]The wise by hearing them will ad-
    vance in learning,
    the intelligent will gain sound
    guidance,
[6]To comprehend proverb and by-
    word,
    the words of the wise and their
    riddles.
[7]Fear of the LORD is the beginning
    of knowledge;
    fools despise wisdom and disci-
    pline.

PART I: PROLOGUE

Proverbs 1:1-7

These verses set out the purpose of the book: it is to be used in learning the full dimensions of wisdom. It will give resourcefulness, knowledge, and discretion to the "simple," those who are young and unformed (1:4), and assist those already committed to the pursuit of wisdom to expand their learning, gain in guidance, and grow in their understanding of wise writings (1:5-6). The sayings and instructions of Proverbs, then, hold out the promise of unfolding the ways of wisdom to novices and the experienced alike.

The qualities of wisdom in which readers will be instructed are varied (1:2-4). The Hebrew word translated "wisdom" in verse 2 is *hokmah*. It means, in a concrete sense, skill developed through experience (see, e.g., 1 Kings 7:14). In Proverbs *hokmah* conveys competence in building a fruitful and happy life. It is linked with discipline in verse 2 and in the concluding line of the prologue (1:7). The word "discipline" implies the active engagement of the student in

II. Instructions of Parents and of Woman Wisdom

The Path of the Wicked: Greed and Violence

◀ ⁸Hear, my son, your father's instruction,
and reject not your mother's teaching;
⁹A graceful diadem will they be for your head;
a pendant for your neck.

¹⁰My son, should sinners entice you,
¹¹do not go if they say, "Come along with us!
Let us lie in wait for blood,
unprovoked, let us trap the innocent;
¹²Let us swallow them alive, like Sheol,
whole, like those who go down to the pit!

learning. It draws out the element of skill and expertise in wisdom. Wisdom has an active component and entails ongoing growth in competence. The parallelism of verse 2 pairs this kind of active learning with the understanding of intelligent sayings, implying that both practice and contemplation are needed to grow in wisdom. The ethical dimensions of wisdom—righteousness, justice, and fairness—are brought out in verse 3, and the more practical virtues of resourcefulness, knowledge, and discretion are named in verse 4.

Verse 7 concludes the prologue by acknowledging that not all are open to wisdom and discipline. There are fools who despise both because fools lack the quality that makes knowledge of wisdom possible: "the fear of the LORD." This phrase conveys an elementary sense of the presence and power of God in human life, and it is frequent in Proverbs. Here it suggests that acknowledgment of divine presence and power is essential to the acquisition of wisdom (cf. 1:29; 2:5; 9:10).

PART II: INTRODUCTION

Proverbs 1:8–9:18

Proverbs 1:8–9:18 forms a sustained introduction to the book of Proverbs. It extols the value of wisdom as a quality of being that transcends particular wise behaviors. The longer literary compositions of the introduction are distinct from the short sayings and instructions that predominate in the body of the work. These longer forms offer a vehicle for persuasive, dramatic, and hymn-like language intended to move the reader to engage in the study of the proverbs that follow.

▶ This symbol indicates a cross-reference number in the *Catechism of the Catholic Church*. See page 119 for number citations.

¹³All kinds of precious wealth shall
we gain,
we shall fill our houses with
booty;
¹⁴Cast in your lot with us,
we shall all have one purse!"
¹⁵My son, do not walk in the way
with them,
hold back your foot from their
path!
¹⁶[For their feet run to evil,
they hasten to shed blood.]
¹⁷In vain a net is spread
right under the eyes of any
bird—
¹⁸They lie in wait for their own
blood,
they set a trap for their own
lives.
¹⁹This is the way of everyone
greedy for loot:
it takes away their lives.

The introduction consists of a series of ten parental speeches interwoven with four poetic reflections on the nature of wisdom. A cluster of specific words of advice in 6:1-19 illustrates the range of wisdom.

The parental speeches share a similar form and familial tone, and they build on one another in laying out for the son a fundamental choice between the ways of wisdom and foolishness. The father impresses on his child the rewards of wisdom as well as its demands. The poetic reflections create a sense of wisdom as a quality so real and present that it takes on human shape and voice. In the imagination wisdom becomes a woman who invites all to enjoy her friendship and protection. Chapters 1–9 as a whole, then, can be seen as a duet of intertwining voices, each lyric in its praise of wisdom: the voice of the father (who represents the older generation) and the voice of wisdom herself.

1:8-19 First parental speech: the way of the violent

This is the first of ten parental speeches invested with the loving concern of the parents for their offspring's safe passage into responsible adulthood. The speeches represent a form of instruction or direct advice, and they have a consistent structure in chapters 1–9. Each begins with an initial address to the son and a plea to listen to the parents' teaching (e.g., 1:8-9), a set of commands and warnings (e.g., 1:10-18), and a concluding summation (e.g., 1:19).

The opening line of this first speech refers both to the instruction of the father and the teaching of the mother (1:8). The father is the speaker, but he stresses the value of the wisdom of both parents. Such parental guidance sets a child apart as especially favored, just as a diadem or pendant are signs of acclaim and adornment (4:9; cf. Song 4:9).

The content of the instruction (1:10-18) has to do with the son's choices in the social or public domain. How will he form a network of friends and associates and construct his livelihood? The parents know the appeal of

17

Wisdom in Person Gives a Warning

²⁰Wisdom cries aloud in the street,
in the open squares she raises
her voice;
²¹Down the crowded ways she calls
out,
at the city gates she utters her
words:
²²"How long, you naive ones, will
you love naivete,
²³How long will you turn away
at my reproof?
[The arrogant delight in their arrogance,
and fools hate knowledge.]
Lo! I will pour out to you my
spirit,
I will acquaint you with my
words:

²⁴"Because I called and you refused,
extended my hand and no one
took notice;
²⁵Because you disdained all my
counsel,
and my reproof you ignored—
²⁶I, in my turn, will laugh at your
doom;
will mock when terror overtakes
you;
²⁷When terror comes upon you like
a storm,
and your doom approaches like
a whirlwind;
when distress and anguish befall you.'
²⁸Then they will call me, but I will
not answer;

"sinners" who grasp at wealth by preying on others, and the father is able to produce a life-like imitation of their thoughts and words (1:11-14). He counters their enticements of riches and friendship ("we shall all have one purse!") with the metaphor of the way, a central image in Proverbs. The actions of the violent and unscrupulous track a way of life that leads beyond the immediate gains of wealth that preoccupy them. It is a path on which their feet "run to evil" as they "hasten to shed blood" (1:16), and it inevitably brings them to ambush and harm (1:18). Verse 19 offers a final pronouncement on this way of life: it is self-destructive.

1:20-33 First poem: Wisdom's lament

Wisdom's own voice now takes over from the father's. Wisdom is conceived as a whole quality of being and appears in the figure of a woman. In this poem she stands in the public domain: in streets and squares and at the city gates, the hub of the city's economic and civic transactions. The city gates are, further, traditionally associated with the hearing of disputes and dispensing of justice by the city's elders (Amos 5:15). Wisdom's appeal to the "naive," or unthinking, thus stands as an alternative to the appeal of the sinners in the previous speech.

Like the father's speech, wisdom's words are full of warning, but they depict the choices facing the young person in broader terms. Here the option lies between responding to wisdom's invitation or turning away from

18

"When terror comes upon you like a storm, and your doom approaches like a whirlwind . . ." (Prov 1:27).

they will seek me, but will not
find me,
²⁹Because they hated knowledge,
and the fear of the LORD they
did not choose.
³⁰They ignored my counsel,
they spurned all my reproof;
³¹Well, then, they shall eat the fruit
of their own way,
and with their own devices be
glutted.
³²For the straying of the naive kills
them,

the smugness of fools destroys
them.
³³But whoever obeys me dwells in
security,
in peace, without fear of
harm."

The Blessings of Wisdom

2 ¹My son, if you receive my words
and treasure my commands,
²Turning your ear to wisdom,
inclining your heart to understanding;

---

her (cf. 1:7b). The choice is an active one that involves transformation from a state of contentment with careless naiveté (1:22).

The question "how long" in verse 22 is characteristic of psalm laments (Pss 6:4, 74:10; 82:2). It occurs also in prophetic speeches where either the prophet or God laments over the intractability of the people of Israel (Hos 8:5, Isa 6:11, Jer 4:14, 21; 13:27). Wisdom's speech here has prophetic resonance as she reproves the simple for refusing her outstretched hand and ignoring her counsel and correction (1:23-25). This scenario of resistance is comparable to the deaf ears and closed eyes that the prophet Isaiah is told he must confront in Isaiah 6:10 (see also Jer 1:19; Ezek 2:3-7). Prophetic, too, is wisdom's foretelling of calamity for those who ignore her (1:26-31). The prospect of seeking wisdom too late (1:28) is reminiscent of the desperate but futile search for the word of the Lord in Amos 8:12.

Wisdom links the rejection of knowledge by the naive to their failure to choose the fear of the Lord (1:29). They have no sense of what is larger than their own experience, and their hatred of knowledge expresses itself in the spurning of all advice and correction (1:30). But they will be compelled to eat the fruit of the way they have chosen (1:31). The final summation in 1:32 is incisive: the turning away from wisdom by the naive "kills them." Verse 33 sounds a final note of hopeful contrast: those who listen to wisdom will live safely and without fear of harm.

2:1-22 Second parental speech: the safe way

The father's voice now picks up the theme of the choice *for* wisdom, and his assurances about the safety of the way of wisdom echo the promise of wisdom herself in 1:33.

³Yes, if you call for intelligence,
  and to understanding raise your
    voice;
⁴If you seek her like silver,
  and like hidden treasures search
    her out,
⁵Then will you understand the fear
  of the LORD;
  the knowledge of God you will
    find;

⁶For the LORD gives wisdom,
  from his mouth come knowl-
    edge and understanding;
⁷He has success in store for the up-
    right,
  is the shield of those who walk
    honestly,
⁸Guarding the paths of justice,
  protecting the way of his faith-
    ful ones,

Verses 1-11 describe the unfolding of wisdom in those who are receptive to it. The path to wisdom begins with openness to the father's words and commands. These are parental commands, not the stipulations of the law per se, although in Proverbs the one often evokes the other (see, e.g., the father's warning against adultery in 2:16-19).

Understanding the significance of the father's teaching entails an active response, as the sequence of verbs in verses 2-4 suggests: turn, incline, call for, raise the voice, seek, and search out. The student of wisdom must go after it, for it is not a given but a precious quality that is not easily acquired, like silver or "hidden treasures" (2:4). Only through persistent effort will the young come to understand what fear of the Lord means through gaining knowledge of God and God's ways in the world (2:5). Although the fear of the Lord is the *beginning* of wisdom, growth in wisdom involves movement toward understanding who God is (1:7).

In response to this movement, the Lord himself grants wisdom (2:8). It is a divine gift to those who are sincere, honest, just, and faithful, and it enables them to *understand* what is right, just, and honest and every path that is good in life (2:6-9). Wisdom enters deeply into the heart and soul of the seeker, transforming him or her (2:10). In Hebrew, the heart is the center of a person's thought, or discernment, and understanding. It includes the concepts of "mind" and "sense" and is sometimes translated with these words. The Hebrew word represented here by "soul" means the whole being of a person, the life force that moves him or her.

In providing counsel for the upright, God shields them from harm (2:7-8). Just so, once wisdom has become rooted in the inner being, discretion and understanding watch over and guard the seeker (2:11). Wisdom in her various aspects is a beneficent force in the life of those who receive her.

⁹Then you will understand what is right and just,
what is fair, every good path;
¹⁰For wisdom will enter your heart,
knowledge will be at home in your soul,
¹¹Discretion will watch over you,
understanding will guard you;
¹²Saving you from the way of the wicked,
from those whose speech is perverse.
¹³From those who have left the straight paths
to walk in the ways of darkness,
¹⁴Who delight in doing evil
and celebrate perversity;
¹⁵Whose ways are crooked,
whose paths are devious;
¹⁶Saving you from a stranger,

Verses 12-19 provide two illustrations of the kind of protection wisdom offers. First, discretion and understanding will save a person, not necessarily from all harm, but from the way of the wicked: from those who "walk in ways of darkness" and whose ways are crooked and devious (2:13-15). The further identification of the wicked as those who "delight in doing evil" (2:14) recalls the sinners in 1:10, whose paths are rife with dangers.

Second, wisdom will save a young man from danger of a more personal nature: the woman married to someone else who is ready to forget her marriage vows. Literally, the Hebrew refers to the "stranger" or "foreign woman," one who is bound to another man. With her "smooth words" she attracts the susceptible but leads them on a path that turns downward. The imagery of death in verses 18-19 evokes, if not death itself, a banished and bereft form of existence that is irreversible. These verses sound a serious warning about the consequences of adultery.

The twin dangers of dishonest wrongdoing and adultery presented in verses 12-19 are representative of the seductive paths beckoning the unwitting. Wisdom guards those who listen to her by delineating those paths.

The speech concludes by recapitulating the metaphor of wisdom as a way: the way of the good and the just (2:20). At the same time verses 21-22 introduce a new metaphor based on the central biblical promise of land. Here the choice is between possession of the land and banishment, the finality of which is a lot like death (2:19). A similar theme runs through Psalm 37 (37:3, 9, 11, 29, 34). This choice also recalls prophetic language about exile from the land as well as restoration of the land (on exile, see Amos 7:17; Isa 5:13; Jer 9:15; on restoration, see Amos 9:13-15; Ezek 34:11-16; Jer 31:1-6; Isa 60:21; 65:9-10). The promise of tenure in the land echoes wisdom's promise of untroubled security in 1:33.

from a foreign woman with her
  smooth words,
¹⁷One who forsakes the companion
    of her youth
  and forgets the covenant of her
    God;
¹⁸For her path sinks down to death,
  and her footsteps lead to the
    shades.
¹⁹None who enter there come back,
  or gain the paths of life.
²⁰Thus you may walk in the way of
    the good,
  and keep to the paths of the just.
²¹For the upright will dwell in the
    land,
  people of integrity will remain
    in it;
²²But the wicked will be cut off
    from the land,
  the faithless will be rooted out
    of it.

Confidence in God Leads to Prosperity

3 ¹My son, do not forget my
    teaching,
  take to heart my commands;
²For many days, and years of life,
  and peace, will they bring you.
³Do not let love and fidelity forsake
    you;
  bind them around your neck;
  write them on the tablet of your
    heart.
⁴Then will you win favor and esteem
  before God and human beings.
⁵Trust in the LORD with all your
    heart,
  on your own intelligence do not
    rely;
⁶In all your ways be mindful of
    him,
  and he will make straight your
    paths.

3:1-12 Third parental speech: what wisdom demands

This speech expands on the theme of divine grace in the conferring of wisdom. The opening address begins by urging the son to keep mindful of his father's teaching and commands because they will safeguard his life, bringing him both longevity and peace (3:1-2). Verses 3-10 then enunciate what taking the father's wisdom to heart demands and what it will ensure. In verse 3 it means wrapping oneself in the parental teachings as if around one's neck (6:21; 7:3; cf. Deut 6:8). The command to "write them on the tablets of the heart" further suggests the inner appropriation that is part of growth in wisdom (2:10; 7:3; cf. Jer 17:1 and 31:33). This will elicit favor and regard on the part of both God and others (3:4).

True wisdom, moreover, demands trusting in God for guidance and being mindful of the Lord "in all your ways," rather than relying on one's own insight (3:5-6). In essence the fear of the Lord means turning away from what is wrong, which preempts any other brand of human wisdom (3:7). This kind of lived out trust in God will bring about healing and vitality, penetrating deep into the flesh and bones, or self (3:8; cf. Gen 2:23).

The command to "honor the Lord with your wealth" in verse 9 refers to agricultural contributions to the temple. Ritual offerings, too, are part

⁷Do not be wise in your own eyes,
    fear the Lᴏʀᴅ and turn away
      from evil;
⁸This will mean health for your
    flesh
    and vigor for your bones.
⁹Honor the Lᴏʀᴅ with your wealth,
    with first fruits of all your pro-
      duce;
¹⁰Then will your barns be filled
    with plenty,
    with new wine your vats will
      overflow.
¹¹The discipline of the Lᴏʀᴅ, my
    son, do not spurn;
    do not disdain his reproof;
¹²For whom the Lᴏʀᴅ loves he re-
    proves,
    as a father, the son he favors.

The Benefits of Finding Wisdom

¹³Happy the one who finds wisdom,
    the one who gains under-
      standing!
¹⁴Her profit is better than profit in
    silver,
    and better than gold is her
      revenue;
¹⁵She is more precious than corals,
    and no treasure of yours can
      compare with her.
¹⁶Long life is in her right hand,
    in her left are riches and honor;
¹⁷Her ways are pleasant ways,
    and all her paths are peace;
¹⁸She is a tree of life to those who
    grasp her,
    and those who hold her fast are
      happy.

of a wisdom founded in fear of the Lord, and they result in productivity (3:10). This instruction overlaps with the prescriptions for worship in the law codes (Num 18:12; Lev 2:14; cf. Neh 12:44).

Finally, those seeking wisdom must accept discipline from the Lord (3:11), which is part of growth in knowledge (12:4). The phrase "the discipline of the Lᴏʀᴅ" represents a way of understanding unforeseen obstacles and hardships as a sign of the Lord's teaching and care. In this respect the Lord acts like parents who correct and challenge the child they love (3:12).

3:13-20 Second poem: wisdom's worth

This poem exalts the full scope of wisdom's value. Wisdom is better than the most treasured tangible objects: silver, gold, and corals (3:14-15). She is, rather, like a living woman who holds out in one hand long life and in the other both "riches and honor." Her ways in the world are imbued with pleasantness and peace (3:16-17). Even more, she can be compared to a tree of life (3:18), an archetypal symbol of earth's fruitfulness in the ancient Near East (Gen 2:9). Those who find wisdom and stay close to her can be called "happy" (3:13, 18). The use of the world "happy" both at the beginning of the poem and at its end reinforces the concept of wisdom as a fortunate mode of being.

The last two lines of the poem (3:19-20) expand the implications of the tree of life as a symbol of creative power, linking wisdom with God's crea-

"[Wisdom] is a tree of life to those who grasp her" (Prov 3:18).

¹⁹The LORD by wisdom founded the earth,
established the heavens by understanding;
²⁰By his knowledge the depths are split,
and the clouds drop down dew.

Justice Toward One's Neighbor Brings Blessing

²¹My son, do not let these slip from your sight:
hold to deliberation and planning;
²²So will they be life to your soul,
and an adornment for your neck.
²³Then you may go your way securely;
your foot will never stumble;
²⁴When you lie down, you will not be afraid,
when you rest, your sleep will be sweet.
²⁵Do not be afraid of sudden terror,
of the ruin of the wicked when it comes;
²⁶For the LORD will be your confidence,

tion of the cosmos. It was by wisdom, understanding, and knowledge that God made the heavens, the earth, and the waters which make life possible (8:22-31; Ps 104:24; Jer 10:12-13). They are engrained in reality as we know it. Wisdom, understanding, and knowledge are the same qualities human beings are encouraged to seek at the beginning of the poem (3:13; see also 2:1-2), and they enable all to comprehend and live fruitfully within the created world.

3:21-35 Fourth parental speech: the particulars of wisdom

This speech begins by drawing attention to two important aspects of wisdom: deliberation and planning (3:21). Exercising these qualities will bring life, grace, and safety to the son (3:22-24). The young need not, then, be anxious about the kind of sudden or unexpected disaster that comes upon the wicked, for the Lord will be their confidence (cf. Job 4:6), keeping their feet from being caught in various snares (3:25-26). This, again, is not a promise that one's life path will necessarily be easy or painless, but that careful thought, along with trust in the Lord's protection, will see one through.

Verses 27-35 comprise specific points of advice that demonstrate the exercise of deliberation in social relationships. The neighbor in these instructions is any member of the community, and the father warns against behavior that irritates or erodes communal relations (3:27-30). Verses 31-32 pose the choice for or against the way of the violent and perverse in this context (cf. 1:10-19; 2:12-15). The behavior of such individuals is disruptive in the most damaging way, and those who adopt it are an abomination, or wholly unacceptable to God (cf. 1:10-19; 2:12-15). The upright, it is implied, contribute to communal harmony and are close to God (3:32).

and will keep your foot from the
snare.
27Do not withhold any goods from
the owner
when it is in your power to act.
28Say not to your neighbor, "Go,
come back tomorrow,
and I will give it to you," when
all the while you have it.
29Do not plot evil against your
neighbors,
when they live at peace with
you.
30Do not contend with someone
without cause,
with one who has done you no
harm.
31Do not envy the violent
and choose none of their ways:
32To the LORD the devious are an
abomination,
but the upright are close to him.

33The curse of the LORD is on the
house of the wicked,
but the dwelling of the just he
blesses;
34Those who scoff, he scoffs at,
but the lowly he favors.
35The wise will possess glory,
but fools will bear shame.

The Teacher as Model Disciple

4 1Hear, O children, a father's instruction,
be attentive, that you may gain
understanding!
2Yes, excellent advice I give you;
my teaching do not forsake.
3When I was my father's child,
tender, the darling of my mother,
4He taught me and said to me:
"Let your heart hold fast my
words:
keep my commands, and live!

The concluding verses of the speech fill out the concept of alternatives with a further set of parallel oppositions between the wicked and the just, the arrogant and the humble, and the wise and the foolish. Similar clusters of oppositions recur in chapters 10–29.

4:1-9 Fifth parental speech: get wisdom

In this speech the father shares his experience growing up under the care and guidance of his own father and mother, thereby heightening the personal tone that contributes to the persuasiveness of the parental speeches. The father insists that what he is teaching his children is good (4:2). It is not his own invention, nor does it represent the experience of his generation alone, but it comes from a tradition of wisdom that he received as a young man from his own father (4:3-4). The echoing of the father's appeal for attention in verse 1 with the grandfather's words in verse 4 illustrates this claim.

The repetition of the injunction "get wisdom, get understanding" in verses 5 and 7 suggests that the speech reduces to this essential point. The verb translated as "get" means to acquire and take possession. It implies active claiming as one's own and may include an element of acquiring

⁵Get wisdom, get understanding!
   Do not forget or turn aside from
      the words of my mouth.
⁶Do not forsake her, and she will
   preserve you;
   love her, and she will safeguard
      you;
⁷The beginning of wisdom is: get
   wisdom;
   whatever else you get, get
      understanding.
⁸Extol her, and she will exalt you;
   she will bring you honors if you
      embrace her;
⁹She will put on your head a graceful diadem;
   a glorious crown will she be-
      stow on you."

The Two Ways

¹⁰Hear, my son, and receive my
   words,
   and the years of your life shall
      be many.
¹¹On the way of wisdom I direct
   you,
   I lead you on straight paths.
¹²When you walk, your step will
   not be impeded,
   and should you run, you will
      not stumble.
¹³Hold fast to instruction, never let
   it go;
   keep it, for it is your life.
¹⁴The path of the wicked do not
   enter,
   nor walk in the way of the evil;

---

through producing or creating (Gen 4:1). The son is urged in the clearest possible language to set his sights on getting wisdom in this full sense. For the young person beginning an independent life and concerned about acquiring many things, from material wealth to community standing to a spouse, wisdom must come first. All that is symbolized by the garland and crown (signs of special favor and recognition) comes with wisdom, once it is won (4:8-9). St. Paul's image of the Christian disciple as a runner straining to gain an imperishable crown recalls the father's advice here (1 Cor 9:24-27; cf. Matt 6:33).

4:10-19 Sixth parental speech: the two ways

In this speech and the next the father develops at length the metaphor of the way, juxtaposing the paths of the wicked and the just as alternative options (4:14, 18). As in previous speeches, the son is instructed with a direct imperative to steer clear of the way of wrongdoers (4:14; cf. 1:15; 3:31). When it comes to the way of the just, however, the father lets his description of it attract the son (4:18). Images of light show that, like the dawn, the promise of this way grows stronger and brighter as one proceeds (Ps 97:11). Not only the end of the way of the just but the way itself partakes in clarity and hope. The path of the wicked, in contrast, is dark, confused, and impassable (4:19). The prophet Third Isaiah uses similar images of light and darkness to characterize the courses of the just and the unjust (Isa 58:9-10 and 59:9-10).

¹⁵Shun it, do not cross it,
 turn aside from it, pass on.
¹⁶For they cannot rest unless they
 have done evil;
 if they do not trip anyone they
 lose sleep.
¹⁷For they eat the bread of wickedness
 and drink the wine of violence.
¹⁸But the path of the just is like
 shining light,
 that grows in brilliance till per-
 fect day.
¹⁹The way of the wicked is like
 darkness;
 they do not know on what they
 stumble.

With Your Whole Being Heed My Words and Live

²⁰My son, to my words be attentive,
 to my sayings incline your ear;

²¹Let them not slip from your
 sight,
 keep them within your heart;
²²For they are life to those who find
 them,
 bringing health to one's whole
 being.
²³With all vigilance guard your
 heart,
 for in it are the sources of life.
²⁴Dishonest mouth put away from
 you,
 deceitful lips put far from you.
²⁵Let your eyes look straight
 ahead
 and your gaze be focused forward.
²⁶Survey the path for your feet,
 and all your ways will be
 sure.
²⁷Turn neither to right nor to left,
 keep your foot far from evil.

4:20-27 Seventh parental speech: the straight path

The father now asks the son to fix his whole being on keeping to a straight path and away from evil. The child is implored again to listen to the father's words and hold them within the heart (4:20-21; cf. Deut 6:6). But more is required: one must guard one's heart carefully, for it is the source of inner sensibility, and from it a life takes shape (4:23; cf. Luke 6:45). Guarding the heart means rejecting what is devious and manipulative in one's speech, keeping one's eyes on the way of life the parent's words trace out (4:25; cf. 4:21), and steadying one's steps in that way (4:26-27).

This speech describes a deep appropriation of parental wisdom that affects how one engages with life (cf. 2:10). In this it is reminiscent of the "new heart" passages in Ezekiel 11:19-20 and 36:26 and the image of laws written on the heart in Jeremiah 31:33.

The opposition between what is upright or straight and what is dishonest or crooked is recurrent in Proverbs (2:13-15; 3:32; 4:11; 6:12; 11:3, 21:8; 28:6, 18). The book of Deuteronomy, further, uses the language of turning aside to the right or left in reference to obedience to the law (Deut 17:11, 20; 28:14).

Warning Against Adultery

5 ¹My son, to my wisdom be
    attentive,
  to understanding incline your ear,
²That you may act discreetly,
  and your lips guard what you
    know.
³Indeed, the lips of the stranger
    drip honey,
  and her mouth is smoother than
    oil;
⁴But in the end she is as bitter as
    wormwood,
  as sharp as a two-edged sword.
⁵Her feet go down to death,
  her steps reach Sheol;
⁶Her paths ramble, you know not
    where,
  lest you see before you the road
    to life.
⁷So now, children, listen to me,
  do not stray from the words of
    my mouth.
⁸Keep your way far from her,
  do not go near the door of her
    house,
⁹Lest you give your honor to others,
  and your years to a merciless one;
¹⁰Lest outsiders take their fill of
    your wealth,
  and your hard-won earnings go
    to another's house;
¹¹And you groan in the end,
  when your flesh and your body
    are consumed;
¹²And you say, "Oh, why did I hate
    instruction,
  and my heart spurn reproof!
¹³Why did I not listen to the voice of
    my teachers,
  incline my ear to my instructors!
¹⁴I am all but ruined,
  in the midst of the public assem-
    bly!"
¹⁵Drink water from your own cis-
    tern,
  running water from your own
    well.

5:1-23 Eighth parental instruction: the deception of adultery

This is the first of three parental speeches that focus on the dangers of adultery (see also 2:16-19). Adultery would have been a common threat to a young man for obvious reasons but also, perhaps, because of the practice of arranged marriages at a young age. Adultery serves as a premier example of the raison d'etre of wisdom because of the strong pull of sexual attraction, which has positive aspects in the right contexts and destructive impact in the wrong ones. Discernment, discipline, justice, and good sense are all called into play in confronting the possibility of violating the marriage of a neighbor. The extended focus on adultery in Proverbs 1–9 enables the readers to view different approaches to critiquing this paradigmatic form of foolishness.

In the opening address of the speech, the father calls the son to listen to his wisdom so that the young man may learn to act with discernment, which is needed because the appeal of adultery (and of the adulteress, or "stranger"; cf. 2:16) is misleading. The parallelism of verses 3-4 is both synonymous, within each verse, and antithetic, between verses. The adulteress's lips are

¹⁶Should your water sources be dispersed abroad,
streams of water in the streets?
¹⁷Let them be yours alone,
not shared with outsiders;
¹⁸Let your fountain be blessed and
have joy of the wife of your
youth,
¹⁹your lovely hind, your graceful
doe.
Of whose love you will ever have
your fill,
and by her ardor always be intoxicated.

²⁰Why then, my son, should you be
intoxicated with a stranger,
and embrace another woman?
²¹Indeed, the ways of each person
are plain to the LORD's
sight;
all their paths he surveys;
²²By their own iniquities the wicked
will be caught,
in the meshes of their own sin
they will be held fast;
²³They will die from lack of discipline,
lost because of their great folly.

---

honeyed (5:3), but her aftertaste is bitter (5:4); her mouth is smooth as oil (5:3), but, in the end, sharp and dangerous as a two-edged sword (5:4). In sum, the steps, or actions, of her way move toward death and the realm of the dead (2:18-19), and the tortuous wanderings of her paths prevent one from even seeing the way of life (5:6).

This is why the father pleads with his sons in no uncertain terms to stay away from her (5:7-8). Dalliance with another man's wife will take all the promise out of life (5:9-11). What the father describes is not simply the social stigma of adultery but the actual damages suffered by one who encroaches on the marriage of another. These include social shame, monetary reparations, and economic deprivation and physical exhaustion (cf. 6:32-35). The father envisions how the son will recognize after the fact that he has ruined his future through willful ignorance (5:11-14). Such visualizations of the end of a pattern of behavior (or of the whole pattern, from beginning to end) are the essence of the wisdom of Proverbs.

The alternative for the son is to delight in his own wife (5:18-19). She is referred to obliquely with images of water (cistern, well, streams, and fountain) in 5:15-17 (cf. Song 4:15). Water is a source of life. If one has such a source, why look elsewhere (5:20)? Why put that source at risk, allowing its waters to be scattered in the streets (5:16)? Although many interpreters have taken the last image as referring to the husband's aberrant sexuality, it is just as likely that this verse refers to the effect of the husband's adultery on the wife and on the integrity of his marriage. A betrayed wife may, in time, turn to others, and her springs and streams, once contained in the well of her home for her husband, will be dispersed outside and shared with outsiders (5:17; cf. 11:29).

31

Miscellaneous Proverbs

Against Going Surety for One's Neighbor

6 ¹My son, if you have become
    surety to your neighbor,
  given your hand in pledge to
    another,
²You have been snared by the utter-
    ance of your lips,
  caught by the words of your
    mouth;
³So do this, my son, to free yourself,
  since you have fallen into your
    neighbor's power:

Go, hurry, rouse your neighbor!
⁴Give no sleep to your eyes,
  nor slumber to your eyelids;
⁵Free yourself like a gazelle from
    the hunter,
  or like a bird from the hand of
    the fowler.

The Ant and the Sluggard at Harvest

⁶Go to the ant, O sluggard,
  study her ways and learn wis-
    dom;
⁷For though she has no chief,
  no commander or ruler,

The end of this speech places adultery within the broader framework of human ways in general: all lie open to the eyes of the Lord (5:21). From that vantage point it is possible to see that the wrongs done by the wicked inevitably entrap them (5:22). The wicked suffer this fate because they learn nothing through discipline, or instruction, and thus fail to grow in wisdom. Rather, by persisting in doing what will bring them serious harm—that is, in great folly—they are lost (5:23).

6:1-19 Interlude: A sampling of wisdom

The four sayings and instructions interjected here serve as snapshots of the path of wisdom and its terrain. The two instructions in verses 1-5 and 6-11 invoke qualities of good sense and enterprise and call the young person to take responsibility for managing his or her own life. The sayings in verses 12-15 and 20-35 address forms of troublemaking and wrongdoing in the community. The interrelation of individual and communal perspectives here anticipates a similar mix in the sayings of Proverbs 10–29.

Although the first instruction begins in verse 1 with the familiar address, "my son," it lacks the overall structure of the parental speeches. It resembles, rather, the shorter and more loosely structured instructions found in Proverbs 22:17–24:22.

Verses 1-5 warn against guaranteeing the debts of a neighbor, or fellow community member. This is a recurrent theme in Proverbs (11:15; 17:18; 20:16; 22:26-27; 27:13). The advice may seem to run counter to other exhortations to share generously with the poor (14:21, 31; 19:17; 31:8-9). It is consistent, however, with the ethos of careful management of one's own resources, which can be seen as a communal value. In effect the warning

⁸She procures her food in the sum-
    mer,
  stores up her provisions in the
    harvest.
⁹How long, O sluggard, will you lie
    there?
  when will you rise from your
    sleep?
¹⁰A little sleep, a little slumber,
  a little folding of the arms to
    rest—
¹¹Then poverty will come upon you
  like a robber,
  and want like a brigand.

The Scoundrel
¹²Scoundrels, villains, are they
  who deal in crooked talk.
¹³Shifty of eye,
  feet ever moving,
  pointing with fingers,
¹⁴They have perversity in their hearts,
  always plotting evil,
  sowing discord.
¹⁵Therefore their doom comes sud-
    denly;
  in an instant they are crushed
    beyond cure.

promotes a healthy realism about taking on someone else's debt. Verse 5 ends the instruction by comparing the person trapped by his or her unwise promises to animals trapped by hunters (6:2).

Verses 6-11 take up an even more frequent theme: laziness (24:30-34 and numerous sayings in chs. 10–29). Here the attention of the lazy person is directed not to a human pattern of behavior but to the ant. An example from the natural world sometimes provides a paradigm against which human life can be seen more clearly (see, e.g., the lists of human and natural phenomena in 30:18-19, 24-28, 29-31). The didactic mode of wisdom remains the same: "study her ways and learn wisdom" (6:6). In this case the ant demonstrates the foresight and hard work that result in a good harvest (6:7-8).

The depiction of the lazy person, in contrast, shows that lack of a work ethic makes one vulnerable to poverty and want (6:9-11). These verses illustrate the adeptness of Proverbs in making general concepts visual through image and metaphor. The reader is shown the lazy person sleeping with folded hands, as defenseless against the intrusion of poverty and want as against robbers or armed men.

Verses 12-15 draw a portrait of the person who is up to no good, showing how one's self as well as one's fate is shaped by a way of life. Here physical features express character and presage destiny. Everything about this person is twisted or crooked, from speech to glance to gait to gesture to thought (6:12-14; cf. 2:12-15). The impact of such a person is to destabilize: to plan harm or evil and to instigate strife (6:14). It is not unnatural, then, that he or she will in time suffer a sudden ruinous twist of fate (6:15).

Verses 16-19 place the preceding description in a theological light: the actions of people set on what is harmful are hateful to God. These verses

What the Lord Rejects

¹⁶There are six things the Lᴏʀᴅ
  hates,
  yes, seven are an abomination to
  him;
¹⁷Haughty eyes, a lying tongue,
  hands that shed innocent blood,
¹⁸A heart that plots wicked
  schemes,
  feet that are quick to run to evil,
¹⁹The false witness who utters lies,
  and the one who sows discord
  among kindred.

Warning Against Adultery

²⁰Observe, my son, your father's
  command,
  and do not reject your mother's
  teaching;
²¹Keep them fastened over your
  heart always,
  tie them around your neck.

²²When you lie down they will
  watch over you,
  when you wake, they will share
  your concerns;
  wherever you turn, they will
  guide you.
²³For the command is a lamp, and
  the teaching a light,
  and a way to life are the reproofs that discipline,
²⁴Keeping you from another's wife,
  from the smooth tongue of the
  foreign woman.
²⁵Do not lust in your heart after her
  beauty,
  do not let her captivate you with
  her glance!
²⁶For the price of a harlot
  may be scarcely a loaf of bread,
But a married woman
  is a trap for your precious life.
²⁷Can a man take embers into his
  bosom,

constitute what is called a numerical saying because they enumerate a list of phenomena that share some feature or features. Such sayings typically begin with a formula that states the number of things listed in a two-part sequence, as in 6:16: "There are six things the Lᴏʀᴅ hates / seven are an abomination to him." This saying elaborates on the statement in 3:32: "To the Lᴏʀᴅ the devious are an abomination." Again, a composite picture approximates the whole person: eyes, tongue, hands, heart, feet (6:17-18). So, too, the propensities described—haughtiness, deception, bloodshed, wicked schemes, false witness, and the sowing of discord—coalesce in the person who is at odds with the Lord.

6:20-35 Ninth parental speech: the foolishness of adultery

The son is urged to impress the father's command and mother's teaching on his mind or heart in the same way that a necklace is tied around the neck (6:21; cf. 3:3). They will then serve as guides and guardians through life (6:22-24; cf. 4:4-6). The imagery here draws on the concept of the amulet, an ornament inscribed with words intended to protect its wearer from evil spirits.

and his garments not be
burned?
²⁸Or can a man walk on live coals,
and his feet not be scorched?
²⁹So with him who sleeps with another's wife—
none who touches her shall go
unpunished.
³⁰Thieves are not despised
if out of hunger they steal to sat-
isfy their appetite.
³¹Yet if caught they must pay back
sevenfold,
yield up all the wealth of their
house.

³²But those who commit adultery
have no sense;
those who do it destroy themselves.
³³They will be beaten and dis-
graced,
and their shame will not be
wiped away;
³⁴For passion enrages the husband,
he will have no pity on the day
of vengeance;
³⁵He will not consider any restitu-
tion,
nor be satisfied by your many
bribes.

The threat to the son takes the form, again, of the neighbor's wife, with her flattering overtures (6:24). This speech focuses on the disastrous consequences of adultery, adding detail to what was suggested in 5:7-14. The teaching of father and mother here emphasizes the inherent foolishness of cultivating desire for a married woman and letting oneself be caught by the signs of her interest (6:25). The relationship between these two steps—desire for what is not yours and susceptibility to desire returned—is perhaps reflected in the saying about committing adultery in the heart in Matthew 5:27-28.

The price paid for adultery is life itself, a cost far beyond what one might pay for a prostitute (6:26). The parents are not recommending that their son seek out a prostitute but explaining the far greater danger of violating a marriage.

The inevitable consequence of adultery is shown by comparison with a natural phenomenon: fire burns (6:27-29). But just as the warning "don't touch" to a child who reaches out toward a hot object is often insufficient, so the father adds another comparison, which shows up adultery as utterly senseless. Thieves may steal out of need because they are hungry and the community still retain some sympathy for their act (6:30). Yet if caught, thieves are held to the communal standard of justice and must repay sevenfold (in biblical idiom, many times over) for what they have taken, even to the point of emptying out their own houses (6:31). The adulterer's act is gratuitous, however, and brings down on him much worse: physical injury, contempt, and a permanent stigma (6:33). These consequences are unavoidable because the jealous anger of the offended husband will seek reprisal without pity and cannot be appeased (6:34-35).

The Seduction

7 ¹My son, keep my words,
   and treasure my commands.
²Keep my commands and live,
   and my teaching as the apple of
      your eye;
³Bind them on your fingers,
   write them on the tablet of your
      heart.
⁴Say to Wisdom, "You are my sis-
      ter!"
   Call Understanding, "Friend!"
⁵That they may keep you from a
   stranger,
from the foreign woman with
   her smooth words.
⁶For at the window of my house,
   through my lattice I looked out
⁷And I saw among the naive,
   I observed among the young
      men,
   a youth with no sense,
⁸Crossing the street near the corner,
   then walking toward her house,
⁹In the twilight, at dusk of day,
   in the very dark of night.
¹⁰Then the woman comes to meet
   him,

The one who commits adultery lacks sense in that he needlessly destroys himself (6:32). Working against such blind self-destruction, the father's command, the mother's teaching, and the reproofs of parental discipline light a way to life (6:23; cf. Ps 119:105).

7:1-27 Tenth parental speech: the tragedy of adultery

Since all the parents' words may not be enough to dissuade the young man from the lure of adultery, the father summons up a lifelike drama before his son's eyes. This scenario of seduction is designed to resonate with the young man's fantasies but also to show their tragic end. In real life the outcome of mutual attraction is not necessarily evident in its initial stages, at least not to the naive. A dramatic narrative makes it possible for the inexperienced to witness the dynamics of adultery at a remove and look at them with a critical eye.

The father's introductory words in verses 1-3 encourage the son, again, to take parental instruction so seriously that it becomes part of his senses (eyes), his actions (fingers), and his understanding (heart). By fully appropriating the father's teaching, the son will in effect claim wisdom as an intimate friend and relation (7:4). The word "sister" is used of the beloved, or bride, in the Song of Songs, as well as in Egyptian love poetry, and it carries associations of deep bonding. The dual bonding of the son with wisdom and with the father's words (7:3) will keep him from being taken in by the "smooth words" of the adulteress (7:5). This advice goes beyond that given in Proverbs 5:18-20, where the son is urged to embrace his own wife. It is through embracing the wisdom inherent in parental guidance that the son will find true and lasting pleasure.

dressed like a harlot, with secret designs.
[11]She is raucous and unruly,
    her feet cannot stay at home;
[12]Now she is in the streets, now in the open squares,
    lurking in ambush at every corner.
[13]Then she grabs him, kisses him,
    and with an impudent look says to him:
[14]"I owed peace offerings,
    and today I have fulfilled my vows;
[15]So I came out to meet you,
    to look for you, and I have found you!
[16]With coverlets I have spread my couch,
    with brocaded cloths of Egyptian linen;
[17]I have sprinkled my bed with myrrh,
    with aloes, and with cinnamon.
[18]Come, let us drink our fill of love,
    until morning, let us feast on love!
[19]For my husband is not at home,
    he has gone on a long journey;
[20]A bag of money he took with him,
    he will not return home till the full moon."
[21]She wins him over by repeated urging,
    with her smooth lips she leads him astray.
[22]He follows her impulsively,
    like an ox that goes to slaughter;
Like a stag that bounds toward the net,
[23]till an arrow pierces its liver;
Like a bird that rushes into a snare,
    unaware that his life is at stake.

In verses 6-20 a vivid scene unfolds. The eyewitness narrative of the father brings the son (and the reader) to a window, looking out at the naive. Among these the father singles out one without sense (literally, "without heart," 7:7; cf. 6:32). This is a young man who is not only inexperienced but lacking an interior life of reflection. He is easy prey for the powerful attraction of adultery. This attraction is personified here, in dramatic fashion, as an adulteress ("stranger" or "foreign woman"; cf. 2:16) in the persona of a prostitute, brazenly soliciting a sexual partner (7:8-13).

She issues her invitation to the young man in verse 14. She has just sacrificed an animal in connection with a vow she has made (Lev 22:21; 1 Sam 1:9-11, 20-21, 24-25). Such a sacrifice, known as a peace offering, was consumed by the donor once the fat parts of the animal were burned on the altar (Lev 3:1-17; 7:11-15). The opening gambit of the adulteress, then, is to woo the young man with the promise of a festive meal.

She rapidly moves on to insinuate much more (7:16-18), assuring him that her husband is out of town and not due home until the end of the month (7:19-20). These inducements are what the smooth words of the adulteress sound like. They are the stuff of fantasy, blocking out any thought of unpleasant repercussions.

²⁴So now, children, listen to me,
 be attentive to the words of my
  mouth!
²⁵Do not let your heart turn to her
  ways,
 do not go astray in her paths;
²⁶For many are those she has struck
  down dead,
 numerous, those she has slain.
²⁷Her house is a highway to Sheol,
 leading down into the chambers
  of death.

The Discourse of Wisdom

8 ¹Does not Wisdom call,
 and Understanding raise her
  voice?
²On the top of the heights along the
  road,
 at the crossroads she takes her
  stand;
³By the gates at the approaches of
  the city,
 in the entryways she cries
  aloud:

But the young man without sense is easily led (7:21). He follows his seductress without hesitation, like an unwitting animal, unaware that what he
is dallying with is his own life (7:22-23). The image of the ox led to slaughter
in verse 22 ironically recalls the woman's invitation to a sacrificial feast.

From this drama turned tragedy the father draws a conclusion in verses
24-27, connecting what has been vicariously witnessed with the "words
of my mouth" (7:24). Unlike the hapless and helpless young man without
sense, the son should exert direction over his heart (7:25). Those who fail
to question or think twice and who succumb to adultery are many (7:26).
But once they enter its realm (the house of the adulteress) they find that it
is anything but festive and fun. Rather, it is the way to the dwelling place
of the dead (Sheol), whose rooms are death chambers (7:27; cf. 2:18-19; 5:5).

8:1-36 Third wisdom poem: the scope of wisdom

The introduction to Proverbs reaches a literary summit in this incanta-
tory revelation of wisdom's reach and roots, most of it uttered in the first
person in her own voice. Much of what has been said about wisdom by the
father and in the wisdom poem in 3:13-20 is declared here by the persona
of wisdom herself, who commands attention as a living reality.

She stands in the center of human interaction and activity: at the city
heights overlooking the road, at the crossroads, at the city gates (8:1-3). But
instead of lamenting over and admonishing those who fail to respond to
her, as in 1:20-33, she appeals to all to learn resourcefulness and sense and
to trust her as a teacher (8:5-9).

She claims to speak honestly (8:6-7), in contrast to the smooth words
of the seductress. Her words ring true to those with the intelligence and
knowledge to understand them (8:8-9). Her teaching is as trustworthy as
sterling or gold, but more valuable (8:10-11; cf. 3:14-15).

39

"[The young man] follows [the prostitute] impulsively, like an ox that goes to slaughter"
(Prov 7:22).

⁴"To you, O people, I call;
my appeal is to you mortals.
⁵You naive ones, gain prudence,
you fools, gain sense.
⁶Listen! for noble things I speak;
my lips proclaim honest words.
⁷Indeed, my mouth utters truth,
and my lips abhor wickedness.
⁸All the words of my mouth are sincere,
none of them wily or crooked;
⁹All of them are straightforward to
the intelligent,
and right to those who attain
knowledge.
¹⁰Take my instruction instead of silver,
and knowledge rather than
choice gold.
¹¹[For Wisdom is better than corals,
and no treasures can compare
with her.]
¹²I, Wisdom, dwell with prudence,
and useful knowledge I have.
¹³[The fear of the LORD is hatred of
evil;]

In verses 12-14 wisdom tells us herself who she is. She claims the qualities of prudence, useful knowledge, counsel and advice as well as strength (8:12, 14). We can infer that wisdom is able to see and assess the realities of life on the ground, however discomforting, and to respond to them capably. In all these respects wisdom embodies understanding of human life: "I am understanding" (8:14).

These are the attributes that enable kings and rulers to make justice a reality for those they govern (8:15-16). But wisdom is not reserved solely for rulers: she loves all those who love her and shows herself to all who look for her (8:17; cf. Wis 7:27-28). To all she holds out her rewards: riches, honor, and wealth (8:18). Yet these standard concepts of well-being are inadequate to express the fruits of a relationship with her (8:19). She moves in the ways of righteousness and justice, and the wealth she bestows on those who love her must be understood in these terms (8:20-21).

Wisdom now reveals her origins in a poem within a poem (8:22-31). The beauty of the cosmic imagination in these verses creates a moment of epiphany. Wisdom's origins are with God (8:22). She was formed by God and brought forth at the very beginning of creation, before the earth was fashioned (8:23-26). She was present when God marked out and set in place the heavens, the seas, and the earth's foundations (8:27-29). According to many interpreters (as well as to the translators of the NABRE), wisdom stood beside God as an artisan (Wis 7:22; 8:6). She is associated with the design and construction of creation, as in 3:19, where wisdom, understanding, and knowledge are used by God to found and sustain the heavens and the earth.

Thus God delights in wisdom, who is described in this poem as "playing," before God and over the whole of God's earth (8:30-31). The Hebrew

Pride, arrogance, the evil way,
and the perverse mouth I hate.
[14]Mine are counsel and advice;
Mine is strength; I am understanding.
[15]By me kings reign,
and rulers enact justice;
[16]By me princes govern,
and nobles, all the judges of the earth.
[17]Those who love me I also love,
and those who seek me find me.
[18]With me are riches and honor,
wealth that endures, and righteousness.
[19]My fruit is better than gold, even pure gold,
and my yield than choice silver.
[20]On the way of righteousness I walk,
along the paths of justice,

[21]Granting wealth to those who love me,
and filling their treasuries.

[22]"The LORD begot me, the beginning of his works,
the forerunner of his deeds of long ago;
[23]From of old I was formed,
at the first, before the earth.
[24]When there were no deeps I was brought forth,
when there were no fountains or springs of water;
[25]Before the mountains were settled into place,
before the hills, I was brought forth;
[26]When the earth and the fields were not yet made,
nor the first clods of the world.

verb "to play" also means "to laugh" and includes the meaning of dancing, singing, the playing of instruments, and rejoicing generally (1 Sam 18:7; 2 Sam 6:5; Jer 31:4). The image of wisdom playing suggests the personification of a quality that celebrates and rejoices in God's handiwork in creation, delighting in human beings, as God delights in her (8:31). Overall, the poem reveals that wisdom is founded in creation as God made it, that she articulates and rejoices in creation, and that she has a special affinity for human beings. She thus provides a link between human beings and the Lord, their creator.

Some scholars find similarities between wisdom's portrait here and goddesses of wisdom in other ancient cultures. Parallels have been drawn with the Egyptian goddess Isis in Hellenistic cults, for example, or to the Egyptian goddess of truth and justice, Ma'at. Yet in Proverbs 8:22-31 wisdom is presented as the first of God's creative works rather than as a separate deity (8:22-23, 27, 30). In the Christian tradition the concept of Christ as the preexistent logos in John 1:1 has been associated with this passage, and it is part of the lectionary readings for Trinity Sunday.

Proverbs 8 ends with wisdom turning to the human children in whom she delights and appealing to them directly, just as the father has done to his son (8:24). She summons them to listen to her, hear her instruction, and

²⁷When he established the heavens,
there was I,
when he marked out the vault
over the face of the deep;
²⁸When he made firm the skies
above,
when he fixed fast the springs of
the deep;
²⁹When he set for the sea its limit,
so that the waters should not
transgress his command;
When he fixed the foundations of
earth,
³⁰then was I beside him as artisan;
I was his delight day by day,
playing before him all the
while,
³¹Playing over the whole of his
earth,
having my delight with human
beings.
³²Now, children, listen to me;
happy are they who keep my
ways.

³³Listen to instruction and grow
wise,
do not reject it!
³⁴Happy the one who listens to me,
attending daily at my gates,
keeping watch at my door-
posts;
³⁵For whoever finds me finds life,
and wins favor from the LORD;
³⁶But those who pass me by do violence to themselves;
all who hate me love death."

The Two Women Invite Passersby to Their Banquets

Woman Wisdom Issues Her Invitation

9 ¹Wisdom has built her house,
she has set up her seven col-
umns;
²She has prepared her meat, mixed
her wine,
yes, she has spread her table.
³She has sent out her maidservants;
she calls

---

become wise. In this harmonizing of wisdom's voice with the father's, the parents' instructions take on universal overtones, and wisdom's, the loving intimacy of the parent. As in 8:4-21, wisdom now affirms from her own mouth what 3:13-20 declares: those who listen to her and are persistent disciples are "happy" (8:33b-34). The choice for wisdom is again as simple as that between life and death (8:35-36).

9:1-18 Fourth wisdom poem: the two invitations

The cosmic self-revelation of wisdom in chapter 8 shifts into more domestic images in the poem that concludes the introduction to Proverbs. The opposition between finding and missing wisdom stated in the last two verses of chapter 8 is developed here in the form of competing offers of hospitality. One comes from wisdom, again personified as a woman (9:1-6), and the other from "Woman Folly," a personification of foolishness (9:13-18).

The imagery of verses 1-6 builds on that found in 8:34, where the disciple of wisdom sits at her gates and doorposts. At the same time, it

from the heights out over the
city:
[4]"Let whoever is naive turn in here;
to any who lack sense I say,
[5]Come, eat of my food,
and drink of the wine I have
mixed!
[6]Forsake foolishness that you may
live;
advance in the way of understanding."

Miscellaneous Aphorisms

[7]Whoever corrects the arrogant
earns insults;
and whoever reproves the
wicked incurs oppro-
brium.
[8]Do not reprove the arrogant, lest
they hate you;
reprove the wise, and they will
love you.
[9]Instruct the wise, and they become
still wiser;
teach the just, and they advance
in learning.
[10]The beginning of wisdom is fear
of the LORD,
and knowledge of the Holy One
is understanding.

contrasts with the house of the adulteress, to which the unwitting are lured in 7:27. In chapter 9 wisdom extends a welcome to all the unin- structed, and she is amply prepared to provide for them as guests. Her house is solidly founded on seven pillars and spacious: the number seven conveys completion and perfection (9:1). As hostess, wisdom has spread her table with meat and wine and sent out her many assistants with invitations (9:2-3). In accepting her hospitality and eating and drinking with her, the naive will begin to leave behind their foolishness and grow in understanding (9:6).

Many of the features of this banquet are standard elements of the meal prepared for a guest in ancient traditions of hospitality (e.g., Gen 18:1-15). The meal itself is a sign of shared abundance and friendship, or good will, but also an occasion for listening, hearing, and the exchange of conversa- tion (see Gen 18:9-15; Isa 55:1-3). In this poem the simple are invited to spend time with wisdom, to partake of her food, and to enjoy conversa- tion with her.

Verses 7-12, inserted between the description of the two invitations, remind the reader that not all will be willing to enter wisdom's house or be glad of her company. Although her invitation includes all (9:4-6), paradoxi- cally, a degree of inherent wisdom is needed to accept her corrections and teachings (9:8-9; cf. 8:9, 17). The nature of this prerequisite wisdom is stated in verse 10: fear of the Lord, or a sense of the reality of God, and knowledge of the Holy One, a sense of the nature of God (cf. 1:7; 2:5).

The possibility of rejecting wisdom's invitation has now been raised. Verses 13-18 pose an alternative invitation, from "Woman Folly." The

¹¹For by me your days will be multiplied
and the years of your life increased.
¹²If you are wise, wisdom is to your advantage;
if you are arrogant, you alone shall bear it.

Woman Folly Issues Her Invitation

¹³Woman Folly is raucous,
utterly foolish; she knows nothing.
¹⁴She sits at the door of her house
upon a seat on the city heights,
¹⁵Calling to passersby
as they go on their way straight ahead:
¹⁶"Let those who are naive turn in here,
to those who lack sense I say,
¹⁷Stolen water is sweet,
and bread taken secretly is pleasing!"
¹⁸Little do they know that the shades are there,
that her guests are in the depths of Sheol!

description of this figure creates an antithesis to personified wisdom in 9:1-6. Woman Folly does not symbolize the foolishness of women, but the quality of foolishness in general, just as woman wisdom represents the quality of wisdom in the abstract. The depiction of Woman Folly soliciting passersby to enter her house in verses 15-17 resembles the solicitations of the adulteress in 7:10-20, but adultery is only one form of foolishness (5:20-23).

Folly is loud and restless (9:13; cf. 7:11). Steeped in foolishness, she knows nothing at all (9:13). Like wisdom, she invites the simple to enter her house (9:14-17). The contrast between the two invitations is obvious and laughable, however. Folly has no assistants to send out but sits at her door and yells like a street vendor. She has prepared no genuine meal of meat and wine but offers bread and water stolen from someone else. Although she insists that there is special pleasure in consuming what is illicit and enjoyed on the sly, one would need to be very simple and foolish to take this bait. Verse 18, the last line, suggests that tragically there are those whose naiveté approaches the willful ignorance of Woman Folly. They do not know that her banquet is no treat, that her guests are ghosts, and that her house is a facade leading to the underworld (7:27).

On this note the introduction to Proverbs ends, leaving the reader with a solemn warning to weigh life's choices carefully and critically. Implicitly, the seeker of wisdom is encouraged to study and reflect on the proverbs that follow as an aid to doing just that. They will guide him or her step by step in considering the intricacies of living wisely. They are the meat and wine that wisdom invites all to share.

III. First Solomonic Collection of Sayings

10 ¹The Proverbs of Solomon:
A wise son gives his father joy,
but a foolish son is a grief to his mother.
²Ill-gotten treasures profit nothing,
but justice saves from death.
³The LORD does not let the just go hungry,
but the craving of the wicked he thwarts.
⁴The slack hand impoverishes,
but the busy hand brings riches.

⁵A son who gathers in summer is a credit;
a son who slumbers during harvest, a disgrace.
⁶Blessings are for the head of the just;
but the mouth of the wicked conceals violence.
⁷The memory of the just serves as blessing,
but the name of the wicked will rot.
⁸A wise heart accepts commands,
but a babbling fool will be overthrown.

THE PROVERBS OF SOLOMON

Proverbs 10:1–22:16

Chapter 10 begins the first of a series of collections of sayings and instructions that provide a diverse texture for the basic choice between wisdom and foolishness set out in chapters 1–9. This initial collection bears the superscription, "The Proverbs of Solomon," and it consists entirely of short poetic sayings. It extends through 22:16 and consists of two sections that differ somewhat in both form and content: 10:1–15:33 and 16:1–22:16.

Despite common elements, each saying strikes its own chord. There are 375 separate sayings in this first collection, and it is not possible to comment on each one. Yet to speak of them only in broad thematic or formal groupings is to miss the wit, artistry, and profundity of the individual saying. This commentary will discuss overall thematic patterns where appropriate, but focus on selected sayings that are representative of the diversity and depth of the whole.

Section One (Proverbs 10:1–15:33)

The proverbs in this first section almost unvaryingly use antithetic parallelism to contrast a characteristic behavior or attribute described in the first half-line with one named in the second. The parallelism creates a set of recurrent oppositions, the most frequent being that between the just and the wicked. The basic choice between wisdom and foolishness is thus posed within a matrix of other choices, including uprightness and perver-

⁹Whoever walks honestly walks securely,
but one whose ways are crooked will fare badly.
¹⁰One who winks at a fault causes trouble,
but one who frankly reproves promotes peace.
¹¹The mouth of the just is a fountain of life,
but the mouth of the wicked conceals violence.
¹²Hatred stirs up disputes,
but love covers all offenses.
¹³On the lips of the intelligent is found wisdom,
but a rod for the back of one without sense.
¹⁴The wise store up knowledge,
but the mouth of a fool is imminent ruin.
¹⁵The wealth of the rich is their strong city;
the ruin of the poor is their poverty.
¹⁶The labor of the just leads to life,
the gains of the wicked, to futility.
¹⁷Whoever follows instruction is in the path to life,
but whoever disregards reproof goes astray.

sity, honesty and deviousness, hard work and laziness, restraint and lack of control, generosity and indifference. Often the contrast between ways of life is yoked to a second contrast between the consequences of each way, so that an overall pattern of act leading to consequence is evident.

10:1-32

Verse 1 situates wisdom, as in the instructions of chapters 1–9, within the domain of the family, where character is formed. The antithetic parallelism of this saying is clear: "wise son" in the first half-line is opposed to "foolish son" in the second, while "glad" contrasts with "grief." The opposition between wise and foolish in this first verse provides a rubric for the various contrasts delineated in succeeding verses, and in particular for the predominant opposition between the just and the wicked, which is introduced in verse 2 and repeated in verse 3.

The first half-line of verse 2 denies the profitability of ill-gotten wealth. It corresponds in aphoristic form to the first parental instruction in 1:8-19. The second half-line asserts that justice delivers what is lasting. Verse 3 brings the Lord into the picture. God does not allow the life of the just to waste away through hunger but actively opposes the greed of the wicked. This verse, moreover, begins with the just in the first half-line and ends with the wicked in the second, thus inverting the order of the contrast in verse 2. This literary structure is known as a *chiasm* (an x-shaped configuration), and it locks the thought in place. Acknowledgment of the divine role in the fates of the just and the wicked further reinforces the significance of this

¹⁸Whoever conceals hatred has
  lying lips,
    and whoever spreads slander is
    a fool.
¹⁹Where words are many, sin is not
  wanting;
    but those who restrain their lips
    do well.
²⁰Choice silver is the tongue of the
  just;
    the heart of the wicked is of
    little worth.

²¹The lips of the just nourish many,
  but fools die for want of sense.
²²It is the Lᴏʀᴅ's blessing that
  brings wealth,
    and no effort can substitute for
    it.
²³Crime is the entertainment of the
  fool;
    but wisdom is for the person of
    understanding.
²⁴What the wicked fear will befall
  them,

---

opposition within chapter 10 (where it occurs in eighteen out of thirty-two verses) and in chapters 10–15 as a whole.

Verses 4-5 introduce and reiterate the contrast between laziness and hard work. In verse 4 the slack hand that creates nothing but poverty is opposed to the busy hand that enriches. Verse 5 returns to a familial setting and offers a concrete illustration: the son who gathers grain during the summer wheat harvest is contrasted with the son who is asleep under the haystack. The first son is a success; the second, a disgrace, or object of public disfavor. As in verses 2-3, the repetition of the contrast in two guises at the beginning of the chapter marks its importance (see also 10:16; cf. 6:6-8).

In verse 8 the contrast between the wise and the foolish is presented in terms of one who listens to commands as opposed to the fool who is busily speaking his or her own mind. Here "commands" has the broad meaning of instructions, like those offered to the son in chapters 1–9 (2:1-2; 3:1; 4:4). The parallelism of this verse is not exact. The first half-line describes the receptive posture of the wise person toward instruction. The second contrasts the foolish talker who will be brought down to ruin, introducing a notion of consequence that is lacking in the first. The second half-line says something a little different and something more. Yet the association of ruin with the fool naturally raises implications for the wise listener: surely he or she will proceed from strength to strength. Further, the notion of instruction, explicit in the first half-line, is present as a backdrop in the second half-line, influencing how the "fool" or careless talker is understood. Such subtle asymmetry, which evokes unvoiced associations, is a powerful feature of biblical parallelism.

The phenomenon of speech is taken up again and again, under various aspects, in the sayings that follow. Such sayings attest to the power of words

but the desire of the just will be
granted.
²⁵When the tempest passes, the
wicked are no more;
but the just are established forever.
²⁶As vinegar to the teeth, and
smoke to the eyes,
are sluggards to those who send
them.
²⁷Fear of the LORD prolongs life,
but the years of the wicked are
cut short.
²⁸The hope of the just brings joy,

but the expectation of the
wicked perishes.
²⁹The LORD is a stronghold to those
who walk honestly,
downfall for evildoers.
³⁰The just will never be disturbed,
but the wicked will not abide in
the land.
³¹The mouth of the just yields wisdom,
but the perverse tongue will be
cut off.
³²The lips of the just know favor,
but the mouth of the wicked,
perversion.

in human relationships. Unrestrained speech, deceptive speech, negative and trivial speech, or mistimed speech are arrayed before the reader in 10:10-11, 13-14, 18-21, 31-32. The positive effects of speech are stressed as well as the negative. In verse 11 the mouth of the just is a "fountain of life," in contrast to the concealed violence of the wicked, which destroys. In verse 21 the just one's lips nourish (literally, "shepherd") many.

In some of these sayings about speech the polarities of wise and foolish and just and wicked occur as well, bringing all three sets of categories into alignment with each other. In verse 31, for example, "The mouth of the just yields wisdom" (cf. 10:21).

Lack of restraint in speech is often linked with lack of emotional self-control, another frequent topic in the sayings. Verse 12 distinguishes between love in action and hatred in action. Whereas hatred stirs up conflict and rancor, love "covers over" or buries the memory of all offenses (17:9). This saying is quoted in 1 Peter 4:8 and alluded to in James 5:20.

Verse 26 is a "like" proverb that captures the essence of a situation in a memorable comparison. The images convey effectively just how irritating the lazy are to those who rely on them for various tasks. The comparisons sharpen one's recognition of this phenomenon, but the implications of the knowledge gained are left to each reader to consider.

By the end of this introductory chapter of the first collection of sayings, certain patterns are established. The wise are repeatedly associated with the just, and logically so, since the just enjoy blessing, joy, and long life. They withstand all challenges, while the hopes of the wicked come to nothing (10:28). Through the juxtaposition of various antitheses, wisdom and justice

11 ¹False scales are an abomination
to the LORD,
but an honest weight, his delight.
²When pride comes, disgrace
comes;
but with the humble is wisdom.
³The honesty of the upright guides
them;
the faithless are ruined by their
duplicity.

⁴Wealth is useless on a day of
wrath,
but justice saves from death.
⁵The justice of the honest makes
their way straight,
but by their wickedness the
wicked fall.
⁶The justice of the upright saves
them,
but the faithless are caught in
their own intrigue.

are associated with other qualities as well: willingness to work, to listen and learn, to speak thoughtfully and honestly. These initial impressions are filled out in the chapters that follow.

11:1-31

Verse 1 represents a type of proverb in which a practice or attribute is declared to be an abomination, thus weighting the typically more subtle contrasting of options (see also 15:8; 21:27; 24:9; 26:25). The term "abomination" is especially common in ritual language, where it marks what is unacceptable in terms of sacrifices and other ritual observances. It is used here in a moral sense of what is unacceptable to God in terms of community practices. The strong language reflects the central role of scales in the doing of business in Israel. Agricultural commodities like grain were measured by weight before being bought and sold. Skewing the scales could mean extra profit for one party but hunger for another. Sanctions against this practice must have formed part of the common ethos of the society, as the altering of weights and measures is condemned in the prophetic writings (Amos 8:5; Hos 12:8; Mic 6:10-11) as well as in the law code of Deuteronomy (Deut 25:13-16). Proverbs 20:10 reiterates this particular "abomination."

Many of the sayings in chapter 11 portray the outcome of dishonest practices wholly within the framework of the contrast between the lives of the just and the wicked (11:3-11, 16-19, 21, 27-28, 30-31; but cf. 11:20). These proverbs do not mention God's favor or disfavor, but draw attention to the inherent malfunction of what is "crooked." The metaphor of the path or way comes into play explicitly or implicitly in several verses. A chosen path or mode of life can be straightforward or devious. One would expect the straight path to reach its destination but the twisted path to wander into undesirable byways and possibly never arrive (10:9). This imagery is latent

⁷When a person dies, hope is destroyed;
expectation pinned on wealth is destroyed.
⁸The just are rescued from a tight spot,
but the wicked fall into it instead.
⁹By a word the impious ruin their neighbors,
but through their knowledge the just are rescued.

¹⁰When the just prosper, the city rejoices;
when the wicked perish, there is jubilation.
¹¹Through the blessing of the upright the city is exalted,
but through the mouth of the wicked it is overthrown.
¹²Whoever reviles a neighbor lacks sense,
but the intelligent keep silent.
¹³One who slanders reveals secrets,

in verse 3: the honesty of the upright or incorruptible "guides them," but the duplicity of the faithless or treacherous misleads and ruins them. In verse 5 the imagery is explicit: the virtue of the honest makes their ways straight, whereas the wicked stumble and lose their footing through their wickedness. In verse 6 the impression of self-destruction is even stronger: in contrast to the upright, whose virtue delivers them, the intrigue (literally, the "craving") of the wicked entraps them (cf. 11:8).

Verses 9-11 consider the impact of the just and the wicked on others in the community. Verse 9 refers to the destructive effect of uncontrolled talk against one's neighbor or fellow community member. Verses 10-11 extend the scope to the public arena. Verse 10 states that a city has cause to be happy when the just do well and the wicked fail. Verse 11 supplements this assertion: the blessing of the upright has power to raise or build up a city, whereas the mouth of the wicked can break down not just a neighbor, but the whole social body. Here again, the reference is to both the positive and negative powers of speech, which can generate life but also do violence (10:11; 18:21). The ancient concepts of blessing and curse represent forms of speech that wield life-giving and death-dealing power (Gen 27:1-39; Num 6:22-27; Num 22:1–24:25; Deut 27:1–28:69).

In addition to sayings that weigh the ways of the just and the wicked are some that speak directly of wisdom (11:2, 12, 14, 29). Verse 12 connects the wisdom attribute of intelligence (see 1:2) with speech toward a neighbor. The openness of this saying allows one to imagine scenarios of both the irritating and the blameless neighbor. The rule of thumb for many sorts of social interactions, it implies, is silence (10:19).

Verse 22 is another "like" proverb. The comparison here is striking, even bizarre. The image of the gold ring in the pig's snout, though taken in part

but a trustworthy person keeps
a confidence.
[14]For lack of guidance a people
falls;
security lies in many counselors.
[15]Harm will come to anyone going
surety for another,
but whoever hates giving
pledges is secure.
[16]A gracious woman gains esteem,
and ruthless men gain wealth.
[17]Kindly people benefit themselves,
but the merciless harm themselves.
[18]The wicked make empty profits,
but those who sow justice have
a sure reward.
[19]Justice leads toward life,
but pursuit of evil, toward
death.

[20]The crooked in heart are an abomination to the Lord,
but those who walk blamelessly
are his delight.
[21]Be assured, the wicked shall not
go unpunished,
but the offspring of the just shall
escape.
[22]Like a golden ring in a swine's
snout
is a beautiful woman without
judgment.
[23]The desire of the just ends only in
good;
the expectation of the wicked is
wrath.
[24]One person is lavish yet grows
still richer;
another is too sparing, yet is the
poorer.

---

from the world of animals, is anything but natural. So, it is implied, is a beautiful woman who lacks judgment. Like a gold ornament, good looks gleam and fascinate, but divert attention from the inner sensibility that ultimately defines a person.

Verses 24-25 add the dimension of generosity to the portrait of wisdom. Generosity has a paradoxical dynamic: it enriches the giver. Luke 6:38 and Acts 20:35 express similar thoughts. In a related vein, verse 26 refers to the commercial practice of withholding supplies of grain from the market so as to keep prices high. The public curses those who do this, but blesses those who forgo extra profit and sell their grain to supply those who need it.

Verse 30 is a classic expression of the association of wisdom with life (see 4:22-23; 10:11). The fruit of justice becomes a tree that bears its own fruit, thus engendering more life (cf. the comparison of wisdom to a tree of life in 3:18; 15:4). The New Testament parable of the mustard seed uses a similar image (Matt 13:31-32, Mark 4:30-32, Luke 13:18-19). The "sage" or wise person thus can be said to exert power over lives.

Verse 31 reaffirms the expectation of diverging outcomes for the just and the wicked. If the just are compensated for their acts in this life, those who are committed to wickedness face unthinkable reparations. This saying is quoted in 1 Peter 4:18.

²⁵Whoever confers benefits will be
amply enriched,
and whoever refreshes others
will be refreshed.
²⁶Whoever hoards grain, the people
curse,
but blessings are on the head of
one who distributes it!
²⁷Those who seek the good seek
favor,
but those who pursue evil will
have evil come upon them.
²⁸Those who trust in their riches
will fall,
but like green leaves the just
will flourish.
²⁹Those who trouble their household inherit the wind,

and fools become slaves to the
wise of heart.
³⁰The fruit of justice is a tree of life,
and one who takes lives is a
sage.
³¹If the just are recompensed on the
earth,
how much more the wicked and
the sinner!

12 ¹Whoever loves discipline loves
knowledge,
but whoever hates reproof is
stupid.
²A good person wins favor from the
Lord,
but the schemer he condemns.
³No one is made secure by wickedness,

12:1-28

Verse 1 presents a complex nesting of facets of wisdom. The first half-line asserts that those who love (and welcome) correction are the ones who love (and seek) knowledge. Correction is part of the process of active learning. The first half-line yokes correction with knowledge; the second contrasts the hater of criticism. Such a person is stupid, or unable to learn. See also verse 15, which speaks of the self-assurance of the fool, and 13:1, in which the wise person who loves correction is contrasted with the senseless (liter-ally, "arrogant") person, who dismisses all correction (cf. 9:7-8).

Verse 4 conveys the vital importance of marriage in life, from the per-spective of a man. A worthy wife is, literally, a "strong" or "outstanding," woman, one who pulls her weight in the relationship and is a true life partner. Such a wife is the crown or garland of her spouse, setting him apart as specially graced (see also 18:22; 19:14; 31:10-31). The image of the crown probably reflects the wedding ceremony as well as signaling honor and favor (Song 3:11). Here the choice of a worthy spouse can be seen as an aspect of wisdom. To choose badly is to become yoked to one who brings disgrace or disappointment that eats into the very bones, or self. The He-brew word for disgrace or shame means a kind of publicly acknowledged failure that is felt as utter defeat (Jer 14:3-4). The phrase "like rot in his bones" recalls the saying uttered by Adam when he first sees Eve in Genesis 2:23: "This one at last, is bone of my bones / and flesh of my flesh." The

but the root of the just will
never be disturbed.
⁴A woman of worth is the crown of
her husband,
but a disgraceful one is like rot
in his bones.
⁵The plans of the just are right;
the designs of the wicked are
deceit.
⁶The words of the wicked are a
deadly ambush,
but the speech of the upright
saves them.
⁷Overthrow the wicked and they
are no more,
but the house of the just stands
firm.
⁸For their good sense people are
praised,
but the perverse of heart are despised.

⁹Better to be slighted and have a
servant
than put on airs and lack bread.
¹⁰The just take care of their live-
stock,
but the compassion of the
wicked is cruel.
¹¹Those who till their own land
have food in plenty,
but those who engage in idle
pursuits lack sense.
¹²A wicked person desires the catch
of evil people,
but the root of the righteous will
bear fruit.
¹³By the sin of their lips the wicked
are ensnared,
but the just escape from a tight
spot.
¹⁴From the fruit of their mouths
people have their fill of good,

image implies the deep rooting of the human person in marriage, and the saying can be read in present contexts from the viewpoint of either spouse.

Verse 10 shows, with telling contrast, that justice is a deep and pervasive quality. The just are sensitive even to the needs of their animals, on whose labor they depend. In comparison, even the *compassion* of the wicked is cruel. The depth of the righteous person is also expressed in the image of the root in verse 12.

Verse 14 breaks with the predominant pattern of contrast and sews together two positive qualities to create a two-dimensional picture. Human speech is productive. It creates "fruit" that satisfies and fills a person with good things, just as the work of one's hands is productive and yields results.

Verse 16 suggests the linking of speech, as well as nonverbal responses, with emotion. Fools immediately reveal their anger, but the shrewd conceal contempt (10:12). The saying stresses the intelligence of such a strategy.

Verse 20 draws out the psychological benefit of promoting peace and well-being (the Hebrew word *shalom* means both). Contrasted with the machinations that fill the hearts of those who plot harm is the joy experienced by those who build positive relationships within the community.

and the works of their hands
     come back upon them.
[15]The way of fools is right in their
     own eyes,
  but those who listen to advice
     are the wise.
[16]Fools immediately show their
     anger,
  but the shrewd conceal contempt.
[17]Whoever speaks honestly testifies
     truly,
  but the deceitful make lying wit-
     nesses.
[18]The babble of some people is like
     sword thrusts,
  but the tongue of the wise is
     healing.
[19]Truthful lips endure forever,
  the lying tongue, for only a mo-
     ment.
[20]Deceit is in the heart of those who
     plot evil,
  but those who counsel peace
     have joy.
[21]No harm befalls the just,
  but the wicked are over-
     whelmed with misfor-
     tune.
[22]Lying lips are an abomination to
     the LORD,

but those who are truthful, his
     delight.
[23]The shrewd conceal knowledge,
  but the hearts of fools proclaim
     folly.
[24]The diligent hand will govern,
  but sloth makes for forced labor.
[25]Worry weighs down the heart,
  but a kind word gives it joy.
[26]The just act as guides to their
     neighbors,
  but the way of the wicked leads
     them astray.
[27]Sloth does not catch its prey,
  but the wealth of the diligent is
     splendid.
[28]In the path of justice is life,
  but the way of abomination
     leads to death.
[1]A wise son loves correction,
  but the scoffer heeds no re-
     buke.
[2]From the fruit of the mouth one
     enjoys good things,
  but from the throat of the treach-
     erous comes violence.
[3]Those who guard their mouths
     preserve themselves;
  those who open wide their lips
     bring ruin.

13:1-25

Verses 7 and 8 address the topic of wealth and poverty, a recurrent theme in Proverbs. Some sayings link wealth to hard work and poverty to laziness (10:4; 12:11, 27), but others simply note the discrepancy between rich and poor (13:23; 10:15; 14:20). Verse 7 describes a type of pretense or delusion driven by the polarities of wealth and poverty. One can act as if rich and yet lack everything, or as if poor and yet enjoy great wealth (cf. 12:9). The saying sets the external appearance of wealth and poverty against the possibility of deeper, fuller meanings.

Verse 11 has a practical slant. A steady habit of economy builds up wealth penny by penny. It stands in contrast to the sudden acquisition of riches, which, without such a habit, are easily squandered (cf. 20:21).

"Those who till their own land have food in plenty" (Prov 12:11).

⁴The appetite of the sluggard craves
but has nothing,
but the appetite of the diligent is
amply satisfied.
⁵The just hate deceitful words,
but the wicked are odious and
disgraceful.
⁶Justice guards one who walks honestly,
but sin leads the wicked astray.
⁷One acts rich but has nothing;
another acts poor but has great
wealth.
⁸People's riches serve as ransom for
their lives,
but the poor do not even hear a
threat.
⁹The light of the just gives joy,
but the lamp of the wicked goes
out.

¹⁰The stupid sow discord by their
insolence,
but wisdom is with those who
take counsel.
¹¹Wealth won quickly dwindles
away,
but gathered little by little, it
grows.
¹²Hope deferred makes the heart
sick,
but a wish fulfilled is a tree of
life.
¹³Whoever despises the word must
pay for it,
but whoever reveres the command will be rewarded.
¹⁴The teaching of the wise is a fountain of life,
turning one from the snares of
death.

Despite the concrete tenor of this saying, it can be read on figurative levels as well.

Verse 12 is a classic example of a saying that addresses the psychological dimension of human life (cf. 12:25; 14:10, 13; 15:13). Like others of its kind, it offers a glimpse of the human condition without moving the reader toward a particular course of action. Nothing is suggested in the saying, for example, about avoiding the emotional hardship that comes from the repeated frustration of hope. In the interplay between the two half-lines, however, something is implied. That hope deferred makes one heartsick is a reality, the other side of which is the new life that springs up when a long-awaited desire comes to pass. In the twin assertions of the verse, neither reality cedes to or subjugates the other. Those who ignore one or the other court the dangers, emotional and otherwise, of ignorance.

Verse 19 draws an implication from the delight of realized desires. As often, the inexactness of the contrast between half-lines speaks indirectly, and the reader is impelled to fill in the gaps. That fools cannot break away from doing harm prevents the fulfillment of their desires. Evil is a subversive quality that hinders fulfillment.

Verse 23 makes an observation about poverty. It states baldly the injustice suffered by the poor without hinting at its redress. In this it differs from

¹⁵Good sense brings favor,
  but the way of the faithless is
    their ruin.
¹⁶The shrewd always act prudently
  but the foolish parade folly.
¹⁷A wicked messenger brings on di-
    saster,
  but a trustworthy envoy is a
    healing remedy.
¹⁸Poverty and shame befall those
    who let go of discipline,
  but those who hold on to re-
    proof receive honor.
¹⁹Desire fulfilled delights the soul,
  but turning from evil is an
    abomination to fools.
²⁰Walk with the wise and you be-
    come wise,
  but the companion of fools fares
    badly.
²¹Misfortune pursues sinners,
  but the just shall be recom-
    pensed with good.

²²The good leave an inheritance to
    their children's children,
  but the wealth of the sinner is
    stored up for the just.
²³The tillage of the poor yields
    abundant food,
  but possessions are swept away
    for lack of justice.
²⁴Whoever spares the rod hates the
    child,
  but whoever loves will apply
    discipline.
²⁵When the just eat, their hunger is
    appeased;
  but the belly of the wicked suf-
    fers want.

14 ¹Wisdom builds her house,
  but Folly tears hers down
    with her own hands.
²Those who walk uprightly fear the
    LORD,
  but those who are devious in
    their ways spurn him.

prophetic pronouncements, yet it shares with them awareness of injustice. The saying conveys knowledge about a pattern of human life that can inform the reader in any number of different ways.

Verse 24 is one of the most well known of biblical proverbs because of its currency in home and school settings throughout the centuries. It takes up the recurrent theme of child rearing (23:13-14; 29:15, 17). Changing cultural mores aside, to insist on a narrow interpretation of this verse is to misread the mode of the sayings in Proverbs. The sayings use figurative language to make their points vivid, and they communicate within a network of comparisons and juxtapositions, not equivalents. In this saying the rod serves as a metonym for the whole concept of discipline, which encompasses correction and instruction generally (13:18; cf. 1:2, 7, 8; 4:1, 13; 12:1). To "spare the rod" in the first half-line is antithetically parallel to "discipline," in the second. But discipline is never simply equated with corporal punishment in Proverbs. See the similar metonymic use of "rod" in the phrase "the rod of discipline" in 22:15.

³In the mouth of the fool is a rod for
pride,
  but the lips of the wise preserve
    them.
⁴Where there are no oxen, the crib is
clean;
  but abundant crops come
    through the strength of
      the bull.
⁵A trustworthy witness does not lie,
  but one who spouts lies makes a
    lying witness.
⁶The scoffer seeks wisdom in vain,
  but knowledge is easy for the
    intelligent.
⁷Go from the face of the fool;
  you get no knowledge from
    such lips.

⁸The wisdom of the shrewd enlight-
ens their way,
  but the folly of fools is deceit.
⁹The wicked scorn a guilt offering,
  but the upright find acceptance.
¹⁰The heart knows its own bitter-
ness,
  and its joy no stranger shares.
¹¹The house of the wicked will be
destroyed,
  but the tent of the upright will
    flourish.
¹²Sometimes a way seems right,
  but the end of it leads to death!
¹³Even in laughter the heart may be
sad,
  and the end of joy may be sor-
    row.

14:1-35

Verse 1 attributes to wisdom the accomplishment of building a house
(9:1). A house, as here and elsewhere in the Old Testament, refers not simply
to a building but to a household of children, extended family, servants, and
guests (11:29; 31:15 and Gen 35:2) and often to an intergenerational family
line, as in the "house of Israel" (Ruth 4:11) or the "house of David" (2 Sam
7:27). The house represents the locus of a way of life, and the whole bent
of wisdom is to create a locus that is stable and generative. In contrast
folly pulls down her house with her hands, or activities, illustrating the
self-destructive potential of those who will not learn wisdom (9:18; 11:26).

Verse 4 seems anomalous in its practical agricultural focus, yet it is comparable to Hesiod's *Works and Days*, which combines wisdom instruction
relating to familial, social, and religious life with specific advice on farming.
This saying should be read in relation to others in Proverbs that encourage
intelligent assessment of life's demands and realities (see, e.g., 13:11, 16).
One might compare this saying with the New Testament parables of the
tower builder and the warrior king in Luke 14:28-32.

Verse 8 can be interpreted as a general affirmation of knowledgeable
choices. The wisdom of the shrewd keeps them conscious of the paths they
make through life and where they lead. In contrast, foolishness is deceptive.
The implication is that foolishness does not foster clear-eyed assessment but
misleads fools about what they are doing and the decisions they are making

¹⁴From their own ways turncoats
are sated,
from their own actions, the
loyal.
¹⁵The naive believe everything,
but the shrewd watch their steps.
¹⁶The wise person is cautious and
turns from evil;
the fool is reckless and gets em-
broiled.
¹⁷The quick-tempered make fools of
themselves,
and schemers are hated.
¹⁸The simple have folly as an adornment,
but the shrewd wear knowledge
as a crown.
¹⁹The malicious bow down before
the good,
and the wicked, at the gates of
the just.

²⁰Even by their neighbors the poor
are despised,
but a rich person's friends are
many.
²¹Whoever despises the hungry
comes up short,
but happy the one who is kind
to the poor!
²²Do not those who plan evil go
astray?
But those who plan good win
steadfast loyalty.
²³In all labor there is profit,
but mere talk tends only to loss.
²⁴The crown of the wise is wealth;
the diadem of fools is folly.
²⁵The truthful witness saves lives,
but whoever utters lies is a be-
trayer.
²⁶The fear of the LORD is a strong
defense,

(14:15; 15:14). Verse 12 qualifies these claims about human self-knowledge by reminding the reader that all are vulnerable to self-deception.

Verses 10 and 13 reflect on psychological realities. Verse 10 acknowl-edges the unique configuration of each human sensibility, which is never fully understood by or replicated in another. This assertion nuances the tendency of Proverbs to point to common patterns comprehensible by all. The idiosyncratic is also a component of human life. Verse 13 recognizes the element of sadness in life, even in moments of laughter. The second half-line links this reality to another: the grieving that comes with the end of joy. In acknowledging the sorrowful and transient in human experience, this say-ing is reminiscent of the wisdom of Ecclesiastes (Eccl 3:1-8; 7:2-4; 9:11-12).

Similarly resigned in tone is the observation in verse 20. Word choice makes an effective contrast here: the poor are "despised" or avoided even by their neighbors or fellow community members, whereas the friends or hangers-on of the rich are many.

Verse 21 evaluates this situation from two different angles. The first half-line flatly states that those who despise the hungry are deficient (or sinners). Those who share what they have and are kind, on the other hand, are "happy." The word for "happy" is used elsewhere in the Old Testament in contexts of divine blessing and good fortune (see, e.g., Pss 1:1-3; 34:9;

a refuge even for one's children.
²⁷The fear of the LORD is a fountain of life,
turning one from the snares of death.
²⁸A multitude of subjects is the glory of the king;
but if his people are few, a prince is ruined.
²⁹Long-suffering results in great wisdom;
a short temper raises folly high.
³⁰A tranquil mind gives life to the body,
but jealousy rots the bones.
³¹Those who oppress the poor revile their Maker,
but those who are kind to the needy honor him.
³²The wicked are overthrown by their wickedness,
but the just find a refuge in their integrity.
³³Wisdom can remain silent in the discerning heart,
but among fools she must make herself known.
³⁴Justice exalts a nation,
but sin is a people's disgrace.
³⁵The king favors the skillful servant,
but the shameless one incurs his wrath.

41:2-4). The saying draws out the implications of one's relationship to the poor for both the generous and the contemptuous. The connection between this relationship and the relationship with God ("their Maker") is compactly stated in verse 31 (cf. 17:5; 19:17).

Verse 25 makes the case for truthful testimony in court (12:17; 14:5; 19:5, 9, 28). This particular standard of honesty is deeply seated in the biblical tradition, as is evident in the programmatic prohibitions against false witness in the Decalogue (Exod 20:16; Deut 5:20), the insistence on at least two or three witnesses in legal disputes in Deuteronomy 19:15, and the narrative of false accusation in 1 Kings 21:8-14.

Verses 29-30 spotlight the value of restraining strong emotion and the danger of allowing it to predominate. The Hebrew phrase for "long-suffering" in verse 29 is literally "slow to anger" (16:32). It occurs in Exodus 34:6, where it is used of the Lord's divine forbearance and mercy. In verse 30, serenity is contrasted with jealousy, which "rots the bones," an expression for deep discomfort (12:4; Hab 3:16).

Verse 28 subjects the institution of kingship to an indirect critique by pointing out the dependence of a king's destiny on the proliferation (and hence well-being) of his people. Verse 35 looks at the relationship of servant to king. Wisdom and ineptitude have particular significance within the royal domain. The king is the dispenser of favor (for astute success) or wrath (for shameful failure). This saying would be particularly meaningful for those working within or for the court.

15 ¹A mild answer turns back wrath,
but a harsh word stirs up
anger.
²The tongue of the wise pours out
knowledge,
but the mouth of fools spews
folly.
³The eyes of the LORD are in every
place,
keeping watch on the evil and
the good.
⁴A soothing tongue is a tree of life,
but a perverse one breaks the
spirit.

⁵The fool spurns a father's instruction,
but whoever heeds reproof is
prudent.
⁶In the house of the just there are
ample resources,
but the harvest of the wicked is
in peril.
⁷The lips of the wise spread knowledge,
but the heart of fools is not
steadfast.
⁸The sacrifice of the wicked is an
abomination to the LORD,

15:1-33

Verse 3 carries the genre of pure observation into the realm of theology. Nothing is hidden from the eyes of the Lord, the first half-line asserts (5:21). The second specifies divine watchfulness over both the wicked and the good. The verb "to watch" used here refers elsewhere to watchmen, whose job is to keep an eye out for danger of all sorts (1 Sam 14:16; Ezek 33:2-3). The "wicked" and "good" represent then not simply types of people but their destructive or constructive activities. Such activities do not go unnoticed but are monitored by God. The similar saying in verse 11 claims that even the realm of the underworld and dwelling place of the dead are open to the gaze of the Lord. These sayings, like others scattered throughout chapters 10–15, cast a theological light on the observations of the sayings as a whole. Theological sayings are clustered at the beginning of the section, in chapters 10 and 11 (10:3, 22, 27, 29; 11:1, 20) and at the end, in chapters 14 and 15 (14:2, 26, 27, 31 and 15:3, 8, 9, 11, 16, 25, 26, 29, 33).

Verse 8 has a prophetic ring, with its evaluation of ritual sacrifice in terms of ethical distinctions (the wicked and the upright). The term "abomination," which carries ritual associations, is used to condemn sacrifice that is perfunctory (6:16-19; cf. Amos 5:21-24; Isa 1:10-17). The parallelism of this saying with the next one in verse 9 suggests that the sacrifice of the wicked is an abomination to the Lord because the "way" of the wicked is abhorrent.

Verse 14 captures an irony of wisdom. The discerning heart (mind) continues to seek knowledge about life and the world. In contrast, the mouth of the fool feeds (literally, grazes) on what is foolish. The opposition of mind

but the prayer of the upright is
his delight.
⁹The way of the wicked is an abomination to the LORD,
but he loves one who pursues
justice.
¹⁰Discipline seems bad to those
going astray;
one who hates reproof will die.
¹¹Sheol and Abaddon lie open before the LORD;
how much more the hearts of
mortals!
¹²Scoffers do not love reproof;
to the wise they will not go.
¹³A glad heart lights up the face,
but an anguished heart breaks
the spirit.
¹⁴The discerning heart seeks knowledge,

but the mouth of fools feeds on
folly.
¹⁵All the days of the poor are evil,
but a good heart is a continual
feast.
¹⁶Better a little with fear of the LORD
than a great fortune with
anxiety.
¹⁷Better a dish of herbs where love
is
than a fatted ox and hatred with
it.
¹⁸The ill-tempered stir up strife,
but the patient settle disputes.
¹⁹The way of the sluggard is like a
thorn hedge,
but the path of the diligent is a
highway.
²⁰A wise son gives his father joy,
but a fool despises his mother.

and mouth, the active seeking of knowledge and the sheep-like consuming of what lies in front of one sharpen this saying.

Verses 15-17 qualify the interpretation of poverty as the result of bad choices. Verse 15 observes that a given material situation is not determinative of one's whole state of being. The saying plays with the multiple meanings of the Hebrew words *raʿ*, which means both evil in the moral sense and what is harmful or onerous, and *tob*, which means both what is morally good and what is pleasant and beneficial. One's days may be difficult (evil), but gladness (goodness) of heart feeds one in abundance.

Verses 16 and 17 are examples of "better than" sayings in which two things are compared by measuring one against the other. These verses qualify the good of material prosperity. If surplus wealth is accompanied either by anxiety or by ill will, it is no longer better than modest means. Verse 17 makes the general evaluation of verse 16 concrete by situating it in the context of the daily meals that are a focus of family life. Good will and affection at mealtimes are of more worth than the richness of the food.

Verse 19 combines a "like" phrase in the first half-line with a contrast-ing parallel in the second. The way of the lazy seems to them like a thorny hedge through which progress is not possible, whereas the path of the dili-gent is a highway on which they move quickly forward. The image of the highway or level road reflects the concept of the straight way pursued by

²¹Folly is joy to the senseless,
   but the person of understanding
      goes the straight way.
²²Plans fail when there is no counsel,
   but they succeed when advisers
      are many.
²³One has joy from an apt response;
   a word in season, how good it is!
²⁴The path of life leads upward for
      the prudent,
   turning them from Sheol below.

²⁵The LORD pulls down the house of
      the proud,
   but preserves intact the widow's
      landmark.
²⁶The schemes of the wicked are an
      abomination to the LORD,
   but gracious words are pure.
²⁷The greedy tear down their own
      house,
   but those who hate bribes will
      live.

the upright (11:5; 16:17). The contrast of the lazy with the diligent in these terms illustrates the multidimensional aspect of wisdom and foolishness.

Verse 22 stresses the communal aspect of wisdom. Plans break down when they are made without consulting others, but succeed when many heads are involved (20:18). This is a particular facet of the emphasis on heeding correction and advice in Proverbs (see 15:31 and 32; 12:15).

Verse 23 extols the delight of well-considered conversation. A person's speech (literally, "the answer of the mouth") can be a joy. The second half-line specifies what kind of speech: a word suited to the occasion ("season"). The art of choosing words well is a wonder over which the proverb exclaims, "how good it is!" (cf. Gen 1:13). The constructive power of words is illustrated in verse 1, in which the mild answer turns back anger, as opposed to the aggravating word. In verse 4 a soothing (literally, "healing") tongue is a "tree of life" in contrast to the perverse or disruptive tongue that breaks down the spirit (12:18). In verse 28 speech is related to careful deliberation. The heart of the just person weighs how he or she will respond, whereas the mouth of the wicked pours forth what is harmful (see 15:2, 7).

Verse 25 conveys in miniature the pattern of divine reversal of human fortunes found, for example, in the song of Hannah in 1 Samuel 2:1-10 and in prophetic texts like Isaiah 65:13-16. Widows were among the most vulnerable members of Israelite society, along with orphans and resident aliens (Exod 22:21-24). Without an adult male protector widows could fall prey to schemes that left them without land and property (Prov 23:10-11; Mic 2:9). The landmark refers to the boundary stone designating an allotment of land. According to the book of Deuteronomy such allotments were inherited within families and were not to be altered (Deut 19:14; 27:17). This saying asserts that the Lord preserves widows' rights against the encroachment of those who seek to enrich themselves. The saying has a less obvious basis

²⁸The heart of the just ponders a response,
but the mouth of the wicked spews evil.
²⁹The LORD is far from the wicked,
but hears the prayer of the just.
³⁰A cheerful glance brings joy to the heart;
good news invigorates the bones.
³¹The ear that listens to salutary reproof
is at home among the wise.
³²Those who disregard discipline hate themselves,
but those who heed reproof acquire understanding.
³³The fear of the LORD is training for wisdom,
and humility goes before honors.

16 ¹Plans are made in human hearts,
but from the LORD comes the tongue's response.
²All one's ways are pure in one's own eyes,
but the measurer of motives is the LORD.
³Entrust your works to the LORD,
and your plans will succeed.

in personal experience than many (although the story of Ruth might serve as a literary example), and its prophetic overtones are unmistakable (cf. Isa 5:8-10; Mic 2:1-2). It sets a pattern of divine protection of the vulnerable (and dislocation of the powerful) for the reader to ponder.

Chapter 15 concludes the first section of "The Proverbs of Solomon." It ends with reminders about the need for openness to correction (verses 31-33). Verse 33, the last verse, brings back the theme of the fear of the Lord with which Proverbs as a whole begins. As in 1:7 the fear of the Lord is linked to discipline or instruction in the pursuit of wisdom. Humility precedes honor (16:19), and to know what you do not know is fundamental to wisdom.

Section Two (Proverbs 16:1–22:16)

These chapters constitute a second section of "The Proverbs of Solomon." Sayings that use antithetic parallelism to contrast opposite types of behavior now give way to instances of synthetic or synonymous parallelism that probe the complexities of a single phenomenon. Comparisons are often made through "better than" or "how much more" sayings, and proverbs are sometimes grouped in short sequences that treat a common theme from different angles. There are some short instructions that use imperative forms in these chapters.

16:1-33

The section begins with a cluster of sayings that acknowledge the ultimate role of the Lord in overseeing and directing human life (16:1-7, 9, 25, 33; cf. 14:12; 15:3, 11). These proverbs speak of the outer limits of human wisdom, sounding a philosophical tone that calls to mind the books of Job

⁴The Lord has made everything for
a purpose,
even the wicked for the evil day.
⁵Every proud heart is an abomination to the Lord;
be assured that none will go unpunished.
⁶By steadfast loyalty guilt is expi-
ated,
and by the fear of the Lord evil
is avoided.
⁷When the Lord is pleased with
someone's ways,
he makes even enemies be at
peace with them.
⁸Better a little with justice,
than a large income with injustice.
⁹The human heart plans the way,
but the Lord directs the steps.
¹⁰An oracle is upon the king's lips,
no judgment of his mouth is
false.

¹¹Balance and scales belong to the
Lord;
every weight in the sack is his
concern.
¹²Wrongdoing is an abomination to
kings,
for by justice the throne endures.
¹³The king takes delight in honest
lips,
and whoever speaks what is
right he loves.
¹⁴The king's wrath is a messenger of
death,
but a wise person can pacify it.
¹⁵A king's smile means life,
and his favor is like a rain cloud
in spring.
¹⁶How much better to get wisdom
than gold!
To get understanding is prefer-
able to silver.
¹⁷The path of the upright leads
away from misfortune;

and Ecclesiastes. Verses 1 and 2 use antithetic parallelism to contrast the provinces of the human and the divine. Each saying offers a different configuration of human senses (speech represented by the tongue, and sight represented by the eye) and internal disposition (the heart and the spirit). In verse 1 human beings make plans in their hearts, but the way they actually respond in situations or answer with their tongues stems from God (cf. 16:9). In verse 2 a person's ways may be pure in his or her eyes, but the Lord is the one who takes measure of the spirit or internal intent, trumping human insight as well as human execution. Verse 3 then sets out a logical conclusion: Give over what you do to the Lord, and he will bring your plans to realization.

Verse 4 offers an assurance with which to consider the existence and persistence of the wicked. The saying asserts that "the Lord has made everything for a purpose" (literally, "for its answer"). The wicked can be seen as "made" or destined for a day of disaster, which will be the divine answer to their lives. God's purposes affect the course of the wicked as they do everything else (cf. Ps 73).

those who attend to their way
guard their lives.
¹⁸Pride goes before disaster,
and a haughty spirit before a fall.
¹⁹It is better to be humble with the
poor
than to share plunder with the
proud.
²⁰Whoever ponders a matter will be
successful;
happy the one who trusts in the
Lord!

²¹The wise of heart is esteemed for
discernment,
and pleasing speech gains a
reputation for learning.
²²Good sense is a fountain of life to
those who have it,
but folly is the training of fools.
²³The heart of the wise makes for eloquent speech,
and increases the learning on
their lips.
²⁴Pleasing words are a honeycomb,

Sayings relating to kingship are more prevalent in the second section of "The Proverbs of Solomon" than in the first. Verse 10 reflects the ideal of kingship in Israel and in the ancient Near East in general. The king was regarded as a "son of God" (Ps 2:7; 2 Sam 7:12-15), divinely anointed to maintain justice and order on earth (Pss 45, 72, 101). He was endowed with wisdom in order to bear this responsibility, as the story of Solomon in 1 Kings 3:3-28 illustrates. This ideal portrait of the king lies behind the saying in verse 10: the king's lips are an oracle that imparts inspired insights, and literally his mouth does not betray justice (see also 16:12-13).

Verses 14-15 concern the actual rule of the king. Like 14:35, they seem to be directed toward those who work directly for him. The special position of the king as God's agent and dispenser of justice on earth shows through in the language of these sayings. The king's wrath is like "messengers of death," his approval (literally, "the light of his face") is life, and his favor is like a cloud bringing welcome rain. Those who work closely with the king would do well to remember these realities and draw reasonable conclusions. The wise person, for example, will pacify the king's wrath (16:14).

The dynamic of human pride is underscored in verses 18-19. The verses are linked by the juxtaposition of "haughty spirit" in 16:18b with, "humble" (literally, "lowly spirit") in 16:19a. Verse 18 may be the most well known of Old Testament proverbs in its adaptation, "Pride goes before a fall." The biblical saying does not insist that pride causes disaster, however (as in 11:2). It leaves that possibility open, but it also suggests that pride does not survive disaster. Breakdowns and stumbling in life put an end to haughtiness (18:12). The saying is enhanced by the emphasis in chapter 16 on the role of the Lord in shaping human outcomes (16:1-3, 9, 25, 33). A major setback in life could be the medium through which a person recognizes this divine role.

sweet to the taste and invigorating to the bones.
²⁵Sometimes a way seems right,
  but the end of it leads to death!
²⁶The appetite of workers works for them,
  for their mouths urge them on.
²⁷Scoundrels are a furnace of evil,
  and their lips are like a scorching fire.
²⁸Perverse speech sows discord,
  and talebearing separates bosom friends.
²⁹The violent deceive their neighbors,
and lead them into a way that is not good.
³⁰Whoever winks an eye plans perversity;
  whoever purses the lips does evil.
³¹Gray hair is a crown of glory;
  it is gained by a life that is just.
³²The patient are better than warriors,
  and those who rule their temper, better than the conqueror of a city.
³³Into the bag the lot is cast,
  but from the LORD comes every decision.

Verse 19 asserts the superiority of humility, declaring that sharing a lowly spirit with the poor is better than dividing plunder with the proud (11:2; 15:33). The word "plunder" carries associations not just of treasure but of violent seizure by the powerful (1:13), and it recalls the kind of self-engineered disaster sketched in 1:10-19.

Verse 29 extends the warning given to the son in 1:8-19 to a more general audience. It is not only the young who are subject to peer pressure. The violent and lawless are apt to allure their neighbors into a way that is "not good." Again, the multiple meanings of "good" (morally upright, pleasant, beneficial) add depth to this saying. Verses 27-28, which directly precede, provide specific images of the negative effects of the scoundrel, the intriguer, and the talebearer: scorching fire and divisions between friends.

In verse 31 the praise of gray hair as a "crown of glory" makes a link between righteous living and the grace of longevity (3:16).

In verse 32 the twofold "better than" stresses the heroism demanded in restraining anger and ruling over one's temper (literally, "spirit"). The kingly associations of the verb "rule" are brought out in the image of capturing a city, as kings led their armies into battle. Those who can rule over their own spirits are then greater heroes than warriors and kings.

Verse 33 concludes the chapter by reminding readers of its opening theme: the involvement of the Lord in all that transpires in human life. Throughout the Old Testament, lots are cast to seek divine guidance in making decisions (18:18; Josh 18:6; 1 Sam 10:20-21; Jonah 1:7). Here the lot may be a metaphor for one's portion of life, as in 1:14. Whatever that portion may be, it is the Lord who determines how it will develop.

17 ¹Better a dry crust with quiet
than a house full of feasting
with strife.
²A wise servant will rule over an
unworthy son,
and will share the inheritance of
the children.
³The crucible for silver, and the furnace for gold,
but the tester of hearts is the
LORD.
⁴The evildoer gives heed to wicked
lips,
the liar, to a mischievous
tongue.
⁵Whoever mocks the poor reviles
their Maker;
whoever rejoices in their misfortune will not go unpunished.
⁶Children's children are the crown of
the elderly,
and the glory of children is their
parentage.
⁷Fine words ill fit a fool;
how much more lying lips, a
noble!
⁸A bribe seems a charm to its user;
at every turn it brings success.
⁹Whoever overlooks an offense fos-
ters friendship,
but whoever gossips about it
separates friends.
¹⁰A single reprimand does more for a
discerning person

17:1-28

Verse 3 makes an implicit comparison between the refining of precious metals and the divine testing of the human heart. This metaphor is used of God's testing of Job (Job 23:10) and of the testing of the just in Wisdom 3:5-6 as well as in prophetic oracles of judgment against the people as a whole (Isa 1:25; Jer 6:27-30; Zech 13:7-9).

One of the key tests of the community's relationship with God in much of the prophetic literature is the treatment of the poor. Although several sayings refer to the active exploitation of the poor (14:31; 15:25), verse 5 speaks in terms of attitude. To look at the poor with disdain is to insult one's Maker, and to rejoice in (and benefit by) someone else's distress is to invite punishment.

Verse 6 expresses the primacy of familial relations. For the old, their grandchildren are their "crown," or emblem of blessing. For children, their parents are their glory: their mark of stature and favor (1:8-9).

Verse 8 spotlights the attraction of bribes as a strategy for making one's way in the world. A bribe seems to work like a magic charm, opening doors at every turn (17:23; 18:16; 19:6; 21:14). Injunctions against bribery are part of the basic standard of behavior in the Old Testament (6:35; Exod 23:8; Deut 16:19; Isa 1:23; Mic 3:11). This saying is framed from the perspective of those who offer bribes. It subtly suggests both the enthrallment of bribery as a path to success and the credulousness of those who practice it.

than a hundred lashes for a fool.
¹¹The wicked pursue only rebellion,
and a merciless messenger is
sent against them.
¹²Face a bear robbed of her cubs,
but never fools in their folly!
¹³If you return evil for good,
evil will not depart from your
house.
¹⁴The start of strife is like the opening of a dam;
check a quarrel before it bursts
forth!

¹⁵Whoever acquits the wicked, whoever condemns the just—
both are an abomination to the
Lord.
¹⁶Of what use is money in the
hands of fools
when they have no heart to acquire wisdom?
¹⁷A friend is a friend at all times,
and a brother is born for the
time of adversity.
¹⁸Those without sense give their
hands in pledge,

Verse 9 comments on an aspect of friendship. The language is similar to that in 10:12 but more specific. The one who overlooks, or literally "covers over" an offense genuinely seeks love or friendship (17:17). Whoever reveals the offense to others, however, estranges the friend.

Verse 14 offers a warning about the dynamics of conflict. The first half-line captures attention with an apt comparison between the beginning of an argument and the release of water, which cannot easily be recovered. The second half-line follows up with a logical corollary: avert a quarrel before it breaks out and something vital is lost (20:3).

Verse 19, similarly, supplies an image to rivet a point. The first half-line links offense to conflict: the one who loves to offend loves to contend. The second half-line supplies an analogy: one who raises a gate too high is asking for its collapse.

Several of the sayings in this chapter characterize the fool. The Hebrew word for fool used here (*kesil*) conveys obtuseness and inertia, qualities that are vividly illustrated in verse 10. A single correction is felt more deeply by a discerning person than a fool registers a hundred blows. A fool is not interested in new knowledge. Not even a barrage of warnings and suggestions has an impact, because the fool's aptitude for receiving them is closed (27:22). The dangerous aspect of this kind of fool is brought out by the dramatic comparison in verse 12: a bear bereft of her cubs is less threatening than a fool immersed in foolishness.

In verse 16, even if the fool has the means to buy or acquire wisdom, he or she lacks the heart or sense to learn it. The second half-line exposes the foolishness of thinking of wisdom as a commodity. Wisdom cannot be

becoming surety for their neighbors.

¹⁹Those who love an offense love a fight;
those who build their gate high court disaster.
²⁰The perverse in heart come to no good,
and the double-tongued fall into trouble.
²¹Whoever conceives a fool has grief;
the father of a numskull has no joy.
²²A joyful heart is the health of the body,
but a depressed spirit dries up the bones.
²³A guilty person takes out a bribe from the pocket,
thus perverting the course of justice.
²⁴On the countenance of a discerning person is wisdom,
but the eyes of a fool are on the ends of the earth.

²⁵A foolish son is vexation to his father,
and bitter sorrow to her who bore him.
²⁶It is wrong to fine an innocent person,
but beyond reason to scourge nobles.
²⁷Those who spare their words are truly knowledgeable,
and those who are discreet are intelligent.
²⁸Even fools, keeping silent, are considered wise;
if they keep their lips closed, intelligent.

18 ¹One who is alienated seeks a pretext,
with all persistence picks a quarrel.
²Fools take no delight in understanding,
but only in displaying what they think.
³With wickedness comes contempt,

bought with money in the hand but is acquired by engaging the heart or mind (2:10; 4:20-27).

The contrast in verse 24 is telling as well. Whereas the face of the discerning person is turned toward wisdom, the eyes of the fool are on the ends of the earth: that is, everywhere else. Of the deeper search to understand what is seen and determine what is of lasting good, the fool is unaware. The implication is that the fool must keep looking but never finding. In this saying there is a hint of the personification of wisdom found in chapters 1–9. The intelligent person's face looks toward wisdom, as if toward a guide and companion.

18:1-24

Verse 2 targets the social isolation and self-absorption of the fool. He or she has no interest in understanding but only in laying bare his or her own mind and heart. Fools, it would seem, are very poor conversationalists, if not social misfits (18:13).

71

"Face a bear robbed of cubs, but never fools in their folly!" (Prov 17:12)

and with disgrace, scorn.
⁴The words of one's mouth are deep
waters,
the spring of wisdom, a running
brook.
⁵It is not good to favor the guilty,
nor to reject the claim of the just.
⁶The lips of fools walk into a fight,
and their mouths are asking for
a beating.
⁷The mouths of fools are their ruin;
their lips are a deadly snare.
⁸The words of a talebearer are like
dainty morsels:
they sink into one's inmost
being.
⁹Those slack in their work
are kin to the destroyer.

¹⁰The name of the Lord is a strong
tower;
the just run to it and are safe.
¹¹The wealth of the rich is their
strong city;
they fancy it a high wall.
¹²Before disaster the heart is
haughty,
but before honor is humility.
¹³Whoever answers before listening,
theirs is folly and shame.
¹⁴One's spirit supports one when ill,
but a broken spirit who can
bear?
¹⁵The heart of the intelligent acquires knowledge,
and the ear of the wise seeks
knowledge.

Verse 4, on the other hand, turns attention to the "deep waters" that one's words *can* represent, for the spring of wisdom is a brook that flows forth into words (4:23).

The temptation to listen to rumors is described in verse 8. The Hebrew verb behind "talebearer" means "to whisper" or "murmur," and it carries associations of disruptive activity (16:28, 26:20; Ps 106:25). Yet rumor is hard to resist. Like a delicious treat, it is swallowed and penetrates into one's inner recesses. How such a diet alters the listener is left to the imagination of the reader. This saying is repeated in 26:22.

Similarly frank is the comparison in verse 9. Those who are casual about their work are akin to those who destroy. Many levels of destruction can be envisaged here, including damage to the lives and well-being of all those affected by poor workmanship.

Verses 10-11 use related metaphors to express different perspectives, creating an interactive juxtaposition. Verse 10 represents the perspective of the just. For them, the name of the Lord is a strong tower that stands out in the landscape, and they run for refuge to it and are kept safe. Verse 11 conveys the point of view of the rich: their wealth is their strong city, in their imagination protecting them as does the city's wall against adversary and adversity. The contrast between verses 10-11 invites the reader to compare the impregnability of the two sources of safety.

16Gifts clear the way for people,
winning access to the great.
17Those who plead the case first
seem to be in the right;
then the opponent comes and
cross-examines them.
18The lot puts an end to disputes,
and decides a controversy between the mighty.
19A brother offended is more un-
yielding than a stronghold;
such strife is more daunting
than castle gates.
20With the fruit of one's mouth
one's belly is filled,
with the produce of one's lips
one is sated.

21Death and life are in the power of
the tongue;
those who choose one shall eat
its fruit.
22To find a wife is to find happiness,
a favor granted by the LORD.
23The poor implore,
but the rich answer harshly.
24There are friends who bring ruin,
but there are true friends more
loyal than a brother.

19 1Better to be poor and walk in
integrity
than rich and crooked in one's
ways.
2Desire without knowledge is not
good;

Verse 12 adds an additional note to this interlinear dialogue. Before a breakdown or disaster one's heart may be inflated with self-confidence, but before true acclaim is won, humility must be realized (16:18; 15:33). The word for humility in Hebrew is related to words meaning "poor" and "afflicted" as well as "humble." Since riches are subject to dissolution (11:28; 13:11), the rich person's confidence in them (18:11) may be shaken, and he or she may experience the humility that precedes real honor (Sir 11:1-6).

Verses 17-19 offer wry observations on a more concrete topic: the settling of disputes between neighbors (community members). Verse 17 accentuates a common dilemma for those hearing the arguments in such conflicts. The argument of the first disputant sounds reasonable until the other starts to probe it. The saying prompts readers to think about not judging too quickly the truth of a matter.

Verse 18 implies that some disputes need a radical or "Gordian knot" solution. The casting of lots can effectively bring disputes to an end, even between the powerful. Verse 19 singles out the intensity of family disputes.

Verse 24 turns to one of the relationships that form the nexus of a person's life. An associate may do one harm, but a true friend (literally, "one who loves") is closer than a blood relative.

19:1-29

Verse 2 reaffirms the value of deliberation, or knowing and thinking before acting. Desire without knowledge is not a helpful motivator to ac-

and whoever acts hastily, blunders.

³Their own folly leads people astray;
in their hearts they rage against the Lord.
⁴Wealth adds many friends,
but the poor are left friendless.
⁵The false witness will not go unpunished,
and whoever utters lies will not escape.
⁶Many curry favor with a noble;
everybody is a friend of a gift giver.
⁷All the kin of the poor despise them;
how much more do their friends shun them!
⁸Those who gain sense truly love themselves;
those who preserve understanding will find success.
⁹The false witness will not go unpunished,

and whoever utters lies will perish.
¹⁰Luxury is not befitting a fool;
much less should a slave rule over princes.
¹¹It is good sense to be slow to anger,
and an honor to overlook an offense.
¹²The king's wrath is like the roar of a lion,
but his favor, like dew on the grass.
¹³The foolish son is ruin to his father,
and a quarrelsome wife is water constantly dripping.
¹⁴Home and possessions are an inheritance from parents,
but a prudent wife is from the Lord.
¹⁵Laziness brings on deep sleep,
and the sluggard goes hungry.
¹⁶Those who keep commands keep their lives,
but those who despise these ways will die.

---

tion, and the one who pushes forward in a hurry is apt to lose his or her footing and miss out.

Verse 3 reveals an irony of flawed decision making. It is foolishness that subverts one's way and upsets one's hopes. But the same foolishness may cloud one's assessment of the blame for failure, as one's heart fumes against God. This saying does not refer to all cases of personal disaster but only to those that have clearly been brought about by thoughtless choices.

Both verses 2 and 3 move easily within the circuit of the saying in verse 8, which captures the essence of wisdom. Those who possess sense love themselves, and those who cultivate understanding will find good things (15:32). The similar saying in verse 16 employs the language of commands with the broader meaning of guidance and instruction (10:8). The opposition between life and death in this verse echoes that in chapters 1–9 between adhering to parental teaching and to wisdom, which means life (3:2; 4:22-23; 7:2), and following the way of the violent and wicked,

17Whoever cares for the poor lends
to the LORD,
who will pay back the sum in
full.
18Discipline your son, for there is
hope;
but do not be intent on his
death.
19A wrathful person bears the penalty;
after one rescue, you will have it
to do again.
20Listen to counsel and receive instruction,
that you may eventually become
wise.
21Many are the plans of the human
heart,
but it is the decision of the LORD
that endures.
22What is desired of a person is fi-
delity;
rather be poor than a liar.
23The fear of the LORD leads to life;
one eats and sleeps free from
any harm.
24The sluggard buries a hand in the
dish;
not even lifting it to the mouth.
25Beat a scoffer and the naive learn
a lesson;
rebuke the intelligent and they
gain knowledge.
26Whoever mistreats a father or
drives away a mother,
is a shameless and disgraceful
child.
27My son, stop attending to correction;
start straying from words of
knowledge.
28An unprincipled witness scoffs at
justice,
and the mouth of the wicked
pours out iniquity.
29Rods are prepared for scoffers,
and blows for the backs of
fools.

which leads to death (1:32-33; 2:18-19; 5:22-23). It also recalls the choice between life and death in relation to the commandments of the Lord in Deuteronomy (30:15-20).

Verse 18 brings equal gravity to the subject of child rearing. The strong wording of the second half-line suggests the inherent difficulty of rais-ing children. The command to the parent to discipline or instruct the child refers here to the formation of character in wisdom. The balancing of hope in the first half-line against death in the second insists on the possibilities latent within any child and any parent-child relationship during the formative period. From the child's side, verse 26 calls shame in the strongest terms upon those who mistreat or refuse to care for their parents (20:20).

The saying in verse 24 offers a devastating (if hyperbolic) sketch of the lazy person, who cannot even be bothered to bring the hand he or she digs into a plate of food back into the mouth. The picture serves as its own warning.

20 ¹Wine is arrogant, strong drink
is riotous;
none who are intoxicated by
them are wise.
²The terror of a king is like the roar
of a lion;
those who incur his anger forfeit
their lives.
³A person gains honor by avoiding
strife,
while every fool starts a quarrel.
⁴In seedtime sluggards do not plow;
when they look for the harvest,
it is not there.
⁵The intention of the human heart is
deep water,
but the intelligent draw it forth.
⁶Many say, "My loyal friend,"
but who can find someone worthy of trust?
⁷The just walk in integrity;

happy are their children after
them!
⁸A king seated on the throne of
judgment
dispels all evil with his glance.
⁹Who can say, "I have made my
heart clean,
I am cleansed of my sin"?
¹⁰Varying weights, varying measures,
are both an abomination to the
Lord.
¹¹In their actions even children can
playact
though their deeds be blameless
and right.
¹²The ear that hears, the eye that
sees—
the Lord has made them both.
¹³Do not love sleep lest you be re-
duced to poverty;

20:1-30

Verse 1 specifies alcohol as an ingredient in foolishness through the literary device of personification. Wine is arrogant, drink a troublemaker. These are strong characters who stand for no opposition and thus, like those intoxicated by alcohol, inherently unwise (23:29-35). Drunkenness as a symbol of communal oblivion and degeneration is also a prophetic motif (Amos 2:8, 12; 6:4-6; Hos 4:11; Isa 5:11-12; 28:7-8; 56:9-12).

Verse 5 is one of a number of enigmatic and philosophic sayings in this chapter. The image of deep waters found in 18:4 recurs here in relation to the intentions or plans of the human heart, which are both profound and hidden. Yet the person of intelligence and sense can draw them up like water from a well. The saying suggests that discernment is needed to access the depths of the heart's wisdom and to make it serviceable in particular situations.

Verse 7, one of the "happy are" sayings, suggests the imitative nature of wisdom. The just walk through life in integrity, and their children who follow after them are happy. In having such parents to imitate, they are fortunate (17:6).

keep your eyes open, have your
fill of food.
¹⁴"Bad, bad!" says the buyer,
then goes away only to boast.
¹⁵One can put on gold and abun-
dant jewels,
but wise lips are the most precious ornament.
¹⁶Take the garment of the one who
became surety for a
stranger;
if for foreigners, exact the
pledge!
¹⁷Bread earned by deceit is sweet,
but afterward the mouth is filled
with gravel.
¹⁸Plans made with advice succeed;
with wise direction wage your
war.
¹⁹A slanderer reveals secrets;

so have nothing to do with a
babbler!
²⁰Those who curse father or
mother—
their lamp will go out in the
dead of night.
²¹Possessions greedily guarded at
the outset
will not be blessed in the end.
²²Do not say, "I will repay evil!"
Wait for the LORD, who will help
you.
²³Varying weights are an abomina-
tion to the LORD,
and false scales are not good.
²⁴Our steps are from the LORD;
how, then, can mortals understand their way?
²⁵It is a trap to pledge rashly a
sacred gift,

Verse 8 offers an icon of the king in his primary role as executor of justice. He sits on an elevated throne, surveying his land, sorting out what is evil with his eyes, and scattering it as if in one motion (cf. 20:26).

Verse 9 points to the complexity of determining the purity of one's own heart. Like a number of others, this saying recognizes that the knowledge of what is good and evil sought through wisdom has limits (14:12; 16:2, 25; 21:2). Human judgment only goes so far.

In light of the preceding observations about the realities and limits of judgment, the assertion in verse 12 assumes greater complexity. From one perspective the saying affirms the role of the listening ear and the seeing eye in gaining knowledge and wisdom. Proverbs exalts the value of listening to instruction, and the sayings, with their sharp-edged depictions of human reality, rouse us to look knowingly at the world around us. God has made both ear and eye, and their activity is part of the divine intent.

From another perspective verse 12 can read as a qualification of the human pursuit of wisdom. It reminds the reader that however active the human eye and ear are in gaining knowledge, the knowledge of God, who has made the instruments of human perception, is immeasurably greater (16:1-2, 9; 19:21).

and after a vow, then to reflect.
²⁶A wise king winnows the
wicked,
and threshes them under the
cartwheel.
²⁷A lamp from the LORD is human
life-breath;
it searches through the inmost
being.
²⁸His steadfast loyalty safeguards
the king,
and he upholds his throne by
justice.
²⁹The glory of the young is their
strength,
and the dignity of the old is
gray hair.
³⁰Evil is cleansed away by bloody
lashes,
and a scourging to the inmost
being.

Verse 24 offers a paradox in the same vein. If the steps one takes or decisions one makes ultimately issue from God, what kind of understanding can one hope to achieve about one's way of life? This saying acknowledges the great unknown that surrounds our circumstances and choices: one can live deliberately only up to a point (16:9). The book of Job shows a man who is mystified about the way his life has unfolded, and the book of Ecclesiastes explores more generally the incomprehensibility of the divine order (3:11; 9:11-12) and the limits of human wisdom (1:12-18).

Perhaps the most enigmatic saying in this chapter is verse 27. The link of human beings to God through the breath is expressed in the creation tradition reflected in Genesis 2:4b-7, in which God breathes into the nostrils of the human creature made from the dust and brings it to life. The saying suggests that the breath of life, which comes from God, has the capacity to search out the inner being of a person as a lamp would do. The saying hints at a kind of synergy with God that is inherent in every person (cf. the first reading of 20:12). Yet this possibility must be balanced against verses 9 and 24 and the second reading of verse 12.

Verse 30 is strongly, even disturbingly stated. Again, the metaphorical mode of Proverbs must be kept in mind. The bloody beating of the first half-line is paired with the "inner scourging" of the second. The saying can be read in light of others that refer to physical punishment as part of the discipline of learning wisdom (13:24; 22:15) but can also be linked to the kind of correction that is felt more deeply than blows (17:10). Perhaps, too, this saying shares the perspective of 18:12, which observes that the human heart tends toward self-aggrandizement before experiencing disaster and the kind of real humility that precedes honor (cf. 15:33).

21 ¹A king's heart is channeled water
in the hand of the LORD;
God directs it where he pleases.
²All your ways may be straight in
your own eyes,
but it is the LORD who weighs
hearts.
³To do what is right and just
is more acceptable to the LORD
than sacrifice.
⁴Haughty eyes and a proud heart—
the lamp of the wicked will fail.
⁵The plans of the diligent end in
profit,
but those of the hasty end in
loss.
⁶Trying to get rich by lying
is chasing a bubble over deadly
snares.
⁷The violence of the wicked will
sweep them away,
because they refuse to do what
is right.
⁸One's path may be winding and
unfamiliar,
but one's conduct is blameless
and right.
⁹It is better to dwell in a corner of
the housetop
than in a mansion with a quarrelsome woman.
¹⁰The soul of the wicked desires evil;
their neighbor finds no pity in
their eyes.

21:1-31

Verse 1 evokes, again, the ideal of kingship. The Hebrew word for "hand" also means "power," "force"; hence the unusual image of the heart of the king like a stream of water in the hand of the Lord. Only the Lord could hold a stream in the hand, turning it this way and that.

The insistence of the saying in verse 3 on the primacy of doing what is right and just over the offering of ritual sacrifices is a familiar prophetic theme (Amos 5:22-24; Hos 6:6; Mic 6:6-8; Isa 1:11-17; see also 1 Sam 15:22 and Matt 9:13; 12:7). The Hebrew word translated "acceptable" derives from the verb "to choose" found elsewhere in Proverbs in relation to wisdom (8:10, 19; 10:20; 16:16; 22:1). This saying is related to others that condemn the sacrifice of the wicked as an abomination (see 21:27 and 15:8).

The dramatic rendering of choices in the "better than" saying in verse 9 (and the similar saying in 21:19) leaves no ambiguity about the value of peace and good will in the family. Better to remove oneself to a corner of the roof (or, in 21:19, to the desert), away from any human interaction, than to be caught up in continual quarrels. Both alternatives are untenable: in one case squeezed into a corner exposed to the elements, in the other struggling to eke out existence in a lifeless terrain. These images convey the inescapable misery of a contentious marriage, though framed from the perspective of the husband. The observational mode of the saying allows various implications. The choice of an appropriate mate is certainly one, but the taking of steps within a marriage to avert chronic conflict is not precluded.

[11]When scoffers are punished the
  naive become wise;
when the wise succeed, they
  gain knowledge.
[12]The Righteous One appraises the
  house of the wicked,
bringing down the wicked to
  ruin.
[13]Those who shut their ears to the
  cry of the poor
will themselves call out and not
  be answered.
[14]A secret gift allays anger,
and a present concealed, violent
  wrath.
[15]When justice is done it is a joy for
  the just,
downfall for evildoers.
[16]Whoever strays from the way of
  good sense
will abide in the assembly of the
  shades.
[17]The lover of pleasure will suffer
  want;
the lover of wine and perfume
  will never be rich.
[18]The wicked serve as ransom for
  the just,
and the faithless for the upright.
[19]It is better to dwell in a wilderness
than with a quarrelsome wife
  and trouble.
[20]Precious treasure and oil are in the
  house of the wise,
but the fool consumes them.
[21]Whoever pursues justice and
  kindness
will find life and honor.
[22]The wise person storms the city of
  the mighty,
and overthrows the stronghold
  in which they trust.
[23]Those who guard mouth and tongue
guard themselves from trouble.
[24]Proud, boastful—scoffer is the
  name:
those who act with overbearing
  pride.

Verse 10 gives insight into how the character of the wicked is formed by their choices. The soul or life force of the wicked longs for what is wrong and harmful, and the correlative is that they do not look on their neighbors (fellow community members) with pity or good will. The parallelism in this saying is synthetic, in that the second half-line completes a thought begun in the first. The parallel structure yokes the two features of the wicked together as if each were an aspect of the other.

The consequences of closing an ear to a poor neighbor are spelled out in verse 13. Those who do not hear the poor will not be heard when they cry out. The saying does not specify who, in this event, will turn a deaf ear to the indifferent: one's neighbors, or God, or both. The language echoes that of Exodus 22:22, 25-26 (cf. Deut 24:15), in which care for the poor—including the widow, orphan, stranger, and debtor—is rooted in the genesis of Israel as the people of God.

The poetic justice in this saying is also apparent in the synonymous parallelism of verse 17. The lover of pleasure and celebration will suffer deprivation, just as the lover of wine and perfume, fruits of the earth's richness, will never become rich. In our modern idiom, you cannot have your cake and eat it, too.

²⁵The desire of sluggards will slay
them,
for their hands refuse to work.
²⁶Some are consumed with avarice
all the day,
but the just give unsparingly.
²⁷The sacrifice of the wicked is an
abomination,
the more so when they offer it
with bad intent.
²⁸The false witness will perish,
but one who listens will give
lasting testimony.
²⁹The face of the wicked hardens,
but the upright maintains a
straight course.

The military scenario sketched in verse 22 is hyperbolic but testifies to the superior power of wisdom over physical strength (24:5). Verse 30, however, reminds the reader that there is no wisdom, good sense, or counsel that can prevail over the Lord. And the military imagery of verse 31 qualifies all human endeavor (16:9; 19:21). The parallel structure of this saying links the horse that is made ready for battle to the larger movement of the Lord's victory. The second half-line does not discount the element of preparation but looks beyond it.

22:1-16

Verse 1 extols the value of a "good name." Simply put, a good name is a good reputation. It means that others trust you, welcome you, listen to you, and remember you (10:7). A name is the reputation of a person that is built up through one's actions and responses over time. Like riches, it has to be earned, but it is to be chosen above them because it is more fundamental and enduring. The language of choice is explicit in the first half-line (literally, "a name is to be chosen above great riches"), and the second adds specificity: it is better than silver and gold.

Among many sayings that point to the inevitable social gap between rich and poor (22:7; 14:20; 19:4), verse 2 lays down a more basic assumption. Rich and poor meet in their common origins: God has made them both (14:31, 17:5).

Verse 3 illustrates graphically the perspective of wisdom. The astute person sees evil or harm coming and gets out of the way. This is not necessarily a depiction of moral heroism but of good sense. The naive person keeps on walking, oblivious to what is coming, and pays the price.

Verse 9 raises up the virtue of generosity. Those who are generous are literally "good of eye," looking benevolently on others, and they themselves will be blessed. What generosity means is spelled out in the second half-line: giving from one's own sustenance to the poor. Other sayings warn against taking advantage of the poor and afflicted (14:31; 17:5; 21:13). This one promotes the positive act of caring for the less fortunate by asserting the paradox of 11:24-25: those who give away what they have will receive blessing (14:21; cf. Mark 12:41-44; Luke 21:1-4).

³⁰No wisdom, no understanding,
no counsel prevail against the
Lord.
³¹The horse is equipped for the day
of battle,
but victory is the Lord's.

22 ¹A good name is more desirable
than great riches,
and high esteem, than gold and
silver.
²Rich and poor have a common
bond:
the Lord is the maker of them
all.
³The astute see an evil and hide,
while the naive continue on and
pay the penalty.
⁴The result of humility and fear of
the Lord
is riches, honor and life.
⁵Thorns and snares are on the path
of the crooked;
those who would safeguard their
lives will avoid them.
⁶Train the young in the way they
should go;
even when old, they will not
swerve from it.
⁷The rich rule over the poor,
and the borrower is the slave of
the lender.

⁸Those who sow iniquity reap ca-
lamity,
and the rod used in anger will
fail.
⁹The generous will be blessed,
for they share their food with
the poor.
¹⁰Expel the arrogant and discord
goes too;
strife and insult cease.
¹¹The Lord loves the pure of heart;
the person of winning speech
has a king for a friend.
¹²The eyes of the Lord watch over
the knowledgeable,
but he defeats the projects of the
faithless.
¹³The sluggard says, "A lion is out-
side;
I might be slain in the street."
¹⁴The mouth of the foreign woman
is a deep pit;
whoever incurs the Lord's
anger will fall into it.
¹⁵Folly is bound to the heart of a
youth,
but the rod of discipline will
drive it out.
¹⁶Oppressing the poor for enrich-
ment,
giving to the rich: both are sheer
loss.

The "foreign woman," or adulteress, of chapters 1–9 appears in verse 14. As in the father's instructions, it is her mouth, or seductive words, that entrap (2:16; 5:3; 6:24; 7:5). In the poetic compression of this saying, her mouth not only leads downwards to the pit that is death, it *is* a pit (23:27; cf. 2:18; 5:5; 7:27).

"The Proverbs of Solomon" closes in verse 16 with a consideration of the inequity of rich and poor that looks at the obverse of verse 9. Enriching oneself by extorting from the poor is as unwise as giving money (possibly bribes) to the rich: both add up to loss and want. This is a suitable ending note for a collection assigned to a king who was legendary for taking seriously his royal commission to ensure justice (1 Kgs 3:9).

IV. Sayings of the Wise

¹⁷The Words of the Wise:
Incline your ear, and hear my
words,
and let your mind attend to my
teaching;
¹⁸For it will be well if you hold
them within you,
if they all are ready on your lips.

¹⁹That your trust may be in the
Lord,
I make them known to you
today—yes, to you.
²⁰Have I not written for you thirty
sayings,
containing counsels and knowledge,
²¹To teach you truly

SAYINGS OF THE WISE

Proverbs 22:17–24:22

A new collection begins here under the heading "Sayings of the Wise." Scholars have found significant parallels between these sayings and the Egyptian wisdom composition known as *The Instruction of Amenemope*, which dates to the twelfth century B.C. or before. Parallels are especially evident in 22:17–23:11, where all but three verses correspond at least roughly to passages in the Egyptian work. Particularly striking is the reference in 22:20 to "thirty sayings." *Amenemope* comprises thirty chapters, and various scholars have divided the material in 22:17–24:22 into thirty discrete units.

The narrator of *Amenemope* presents himself as a royal official and scribe who wishes to instruct his son in the skills of a courtier as well as to guide him "in the ways of life," assuring his prosperity and steering him away from evil. The conclusion to the work suggests additional audiences: the inexperienced generally and scribes who aspire to higher positions within the court.

"Sayings of the Wise," in contrast, is not specifically designated for the training of royal officials. These verses, however, contain advice that could be useful to those working with the king or holding positions of power (22:22–23:11). The reference to learning how to give a "dependable report" in verse 21 occurs in the preface to *Amenemope* in connection with courtly skills. Further, the concluding verse of "Sayings of the Wise" yokes fear of the king with fear of the Lord (24:21).

There are also similarities in literary form between these two works. Like *Amenemope* (and in distinction to "The Proverbs of Solomon"), "Sayings of the Wise" largely consists of specific directives or instructions. These frequently occur, as in *Amenemope*, in a two-verse sequence in which the second verse provides a rationale for the instruction in the first. Clusters of

how to give a dependable report
to one who sends you?
²²Do not rob the poor because they
are poor,
nor crush the needy at the gate;
²³For the LORD will defend their
cause,
and will plunder those who
plunder them.
²⁴Do not be friendly with hotheads,

nor associate with the wrathful,
²⁵Lest you learn their ways,
and become ensnared.
²⁶Do not be one of those who give
their hand in pledge,
those who become surety for
debts;
²⁷For if you are unable to pay,
your bed will be taken from
under you.

---

related directives and extended instructions, both of which are characteristic of *Amenemope*, are also evident.

The authors and editors of 22:17–24:22 have by no means replicated the Egyptian work, however. They have adopted the concept of a handbook suitable for instructing the young (including future leaders), expressed some common concerns, and contributed their own reflections, especially in 23:12–24:22.

22:17-22

Verses 17-21 serve as a prologue to the "Words of the Wise," corresponding closely to chapter 1 of *Amenemope*. In verse 17 the invitation to incline the ear, listen, and attend to what is taught resembles the calls to attention that introduce many of the instructions in chapters 1–9 (see, e.g., 1:8; 2:1-2; 4:1, 10; 5:1-2, 7).

The instructions begin in verses 22-23 with a two-verse admonition against robbing the poor that corresponds to the beginning of chapter 2 in *Amenemope*. After this point the order of topics taken up in the two works diverges.

Verses 24-25 and 26-27 are also examples of two-verse admonitions, each of which begins with an imperative in the first half-line followed by an explanation or motivation in the second. Verse 27, for example, expresses in a single image why one should heed the directive in verse 26 against guaranteeing another's loan. You might lose your bed, becoming a debtor like the one you were trying to help—or like the one described in Exodus 22:25-26, who has only a cloak to lie on. Entanglement in the debts of others is a frequent topic in Proverbs (6:1-5; 11:15; 17:18; 20:16; 27:13; cf. Sir 29:14-20).

In verse 28, the "ancient landmark" set up by one's ancestors refers to the boundaries marking land owned by a family and passed on within it (Deut 19:14; 27:17). Stripping people of their legacy of land left them without

²⁸Do not remove the ancient landmark
   that your ancestors set up.
²⁹Do you see those skilled at their
   work?
   They will stand in the presence
      of kings,
   but not in the presence of the
      obscure.

23 ¹When you sit down to dine
      with a ruler,
   mark well the one who is before
      you;
²Stick the knife in your gullet
   if you have a ravenous appetite.
³Do not desire his delicacies;
   it is food that deceives.

⁴Do not wear yourself out to gain
   wealth,
   cease to be worried about it;
⁵When your glance flits to it, it is
   gone!
   For assuredly it grows wings,
   like the eagle that flies toward
      heaven.
⁶Do not take food with unwilling
   hosts,
   and do not desire their delicacies;
⁷For like something stuck in the
   throat is that food.
"Eat and drink," they say to you,
   but their hearts are not with you;
⁸The little you have eaten you will
   vomit up,

---

resources and often drove them into slavery. The prophetic denunciations of such practices in, for example, Micah 2:1-2 and Isaiah 5:8-10 suggest that they were a common occurrence in the preexilic period (see also the narrative of 1 Kgs 21:1-29). Nehemiah 5:3-13 testifies to similar trends in postexilic Judah. Proverbs 23:10-11 echoes this admonition and indicates a particular type of land seizure: the fields of defenseless orphans (cf. 15:25). The dislocation of landmarks is also addressed in chapter 6 of *Amenemope*.

Verse 29 promises promotion to those who develop skill in their work. Promotion will mean serving directly under the king rather than under lesser figures. This saying points ahead to the opening verses of chapter 23, which elaborate on the fine points of working closely with a ruler.

23:1-35

Verses 1-3 address the situation of those who move within the close circle of a ruler or political leader. They take up the subject of proper protocol at official meals, such as state banquets. The advice is politic: (1) keep in mind where you are, or "who is before you," as well as what food is set before you; (2) guard your manners and consume in moderation; and (3) don't forget who *you* are by developing a taste for regal fare. Such food is deceptive: merely emulating the lifestyle of a ruler does not make one more powerful.

This last warning leads easily into verses 4-5, which caution against wearing oneself out in the pursuit of wealth. Chapter 7 in *Amenemope* uses

and you will have wasted your agreeable words.
[9]Do not speak in the hearing of fools;
they will despise the wisdom of your words.
[10]Do not remove the ancient landmark,
nor invade the fields of the fatherless;

[11]For their redeemer is strong;
he will defend their cause against you.
[12]Apply your heart to instruction,
and your ear to words of knowledge.
[13]Do not withhold discipline from youths;
if you beat them with the rod, they will not die.

---

a similar image of riches taking wings like a bird flying toward heaven. In verses 6-8 the discussion returns to the sharing of meals, this time with unwilling hosts (literally, the "evil of eye" as opposed to the "good of eye," or generous, in 22:9). Reading these verses in the context of verses 4-5, the reluctant hosts might be envisioned as those whose eyes have flown toward riches. In any case, their hospitality is poor.

Verse 9 urges discretion in conversation with fools (cf. the warning against throwing pearls before swine in Matt 7:6), and verses 10-11 return to the issue of appropriating land, a temptation to those holding power.

Taken as a whole, the sayings in 22:17–23:11 can be seen as a guide for those seeking or assuming leadership roles in the community. They warn against abusing or squandering advantage and advise on how to deal prudently with problematic characters (fools) and to interface with the powerful.

The admonitions and instructions in 23:12–24:22 have no exact parallels in *Amenemope*. This section of "Sayings of the Wise" resembles the parental instructions of chapters 1–9. The frequent use of the address "my son" and the references to the father and mother of the listener (23:22-25) create an intimate tone. Although different points are taken up, the entire unit flows like one long sequence. It begins in verse 12 with the characteristic appeal to apply the heart to discipline and the ears to words of knowledge. It ends in 24:21-22 with a summative counsel.

Proverbs 23:13-18 consists of three two-verse sayings: two admonitions and a personal appeal. Verses 13-14 address the listener as a parent and speak of the discipline required to raise children intentionally. Verses 15-16 address the listener as a son, who through his wisdom and integrity can bring deep joy to his father. These two sayings culminate in the instruction of verses 17-18. Verse 17 directs the son to guard against emulation of sinners and keep his focus on the fear of the Lord. It suggests an experience

87

"For assuredly [wealth] grows wings, like the eagle that flies toward heaven" (Prov 23:5).

¹⁴Beat them with the rod,
    and you will save them from
        Sheol.
¹⁵My son, if your heart is wise,
    my heart also will rejoice;
¹⁶And my inmost being will exult,
    when your lips speak what is
        right.
¹⁷Do not let your heart envy sin-
    ners,
    but only those who always fear
        the LORD;
¹⁸For you will surely have a future,
    and your hope will not be cut
        off.
¹⁹Hear, my son, and be wise,
    and guide your heart in the
        right way.

²⁰Do not join with wine bibbers,
    nor with those who glut them-
        selves on meat.
²¹For drunkards and gluttons come
    to poverty,
    and lazing about clothes one in
        rags.
²²Listen to your father who begot
    you,
    do not despise your mother
        when she is old.
²³Buy truth and do not sell:
    wisdom, instruction, under-
        standing!
²⁴The father of a just person will
    exult greatly;
    whoever begets a wise son will
        rejoice in him.

of hardship in which it is tempting to follow the model of the successful. Hence verse 18 encourages the son to think about the long term: "for you will surely have a future." In this future the Lord will not disappoint. The envy of wrongdoers is a topic that is resumed in 24:1-2, 19-20 and dwelt on at length in Job 24:1-25, Wisdom 1–5, and Psalms 37 and 73.

A new instruction begins in verse 19 with the call to "Hear, my son, and be wise." Verses 20-21 warn against over-consumption of food and drink, which represent youthful excess generally. The daze created by overindulgence clouds one's potential and in the end leaves one clothed only in rags. The theme of drunkenness is taken further in verses 29-35, and the instructions that lie between these two sections are drawn into relation with the warnings against excessive consumption. This kind of literary bracketing is known as an *inclusio*.

The instruction in verses 22-25, introduced by the plea to listen to both one's father and mother, lifts up a positive principle: what the child should invest in or "buy" is the full range of wisdom qualities: truth, wisdom, discipline, and understanding. These should not be sold or exchanged for anything else (3:13-18). The instruction ends with an appeal to the affection of the son for his parents, especially for his mother: "Let her who bore you exult" (23:25).

An invitation to give one's heart and attention to the ways, or example, of the parent begins the next instruction in verses 26-28. The concern here is

²⁵Let your father and mother rejoice;
let her who bore you exult.
²⁶My son, give me your heart,
and let your eyes keep to my ways,
²⁷For the harlot is a deep pit,
and the foreign woman a narrow well;
²⁸Yes, she lies in wait like a robber,
and increases the number of the faithless.
²⁹Who scream? Who shout?
Who have strife? Who have anxiety?
Who have wounds for nothing?
Who have bleary eyes?
³⁰Whoever linger long over wine,
whoever go around quaffing wine.
³¹Do not look on the wine when it is red,
when it sparkles in the cup.
It goes down smoothly,
³²but in the end it bites like a serpent,
and stings like an adder.
³³Your eyes behold strange sights,
and your heart utters incoherent things;
³⁴You are like one sleeping on the high seas,
sprawled at the top of the mast.
³⁵"They struck me, but it did not pain me;
they beat me, but I did not feel it.
When can I get up,
when can I go out and get more?"

24 ¹Do not envy the wicked,
nor desire to be with them;
²For their hearts plot violence,
and their lips speak of foul play.
³By wisdom a house is built,
by understanding it is established;

---

sexual indulgence, which is represented by the images of the harlot and the adulteress (the "foreign woman"). As in 22:14, such women are a disaster: a "deep pit" and a "narrow well." As in 7:12, they lie in ambush to entrap young men and so add to the number of the faithless or treacherous.

Verses 29-35 return to the subject of alcohol, characterizing the serious drinker as both volatile and vulnerable (23:29-30) and giving a realistic impression of the physical state of drunkenness (23:31-34). The one who suffers all these pains and still asks for another drink is exposed as a sad case (23:35). Although verse 31 explicitly directs the reader to avoid wine, the description of the drinker that follows is eloquent warning in itself.

24:1-22

Verses 1-20 are framed by the matching warnings in verses 1-2 and 19-20 against the envy of wrongdoers (cf. 23:17-18). What lies between these two endpoints can be seen in relation to them (another example of *inclusio*).

Following the initial directive not to emulate or seek out wrongdoers, since they cause havoc and harm, verses 3-4 assert that a house or habitat

⁴And by knowledge its rooms are
filled
with every precious and pleasing possession.
⁵The wise are more powerful than
the strong,
and the learned, than the
mighty,
⁶For by strategy war is waged,
and victory depends on many
counselors.
⁷Wise words are beyond fools'
reach,
in the assembly they do not
open their mouth;
⁸As they calculate how to do evil,
people brand them troublemakers.
⁹The scheme of a fool gains no acceptance,
the scoffer is an abomination to
the community.
¹⁰Did you fail in a day of adversity,
did your strength fall short?

¹¹Did you fail to rescue those who
were being dragged off to
death,
those tottering, those near
death,
¹²because you said, "We didn't
know about it"?
Surely, the Searcher of hearts knows
and will repay all according to
their deeds.
¹³If you eat honey, my son, because
it is good,
if pure honey is sweet to your
taste,
¹⁴Such, you must know, is wisdom
to your soul.
If you find it, you will have a future,
and your hope will not be cut
off.
¹⁵Do not lie in wait at the abode of
the just,
do not ravage their dwelling
places;

is constructed, made firm, and enriched by wisdom, understanding, and knowledge (9:1-6). Similarly, in verses 5-6 battles are won by planning and much consultation (20:18; 21:22).

Foolishness, on the other hand, hinders one's effectiveness in the community, as verses 7-9 make clear. In verse 7 the assembly refers to the gathering of elders at the city gate to conduct civic business (Ruth 4:1-12). Fools are hampered in this arena by their lack of wisdom, which keeps them silent. Verse 8 observes that one who consistently schemes to bring about what is wrong and harmful becomes labeled as such, and is presumably avoided by others. Verse 9 concludes that above all other manifestations of harmful foolishness, the arrogant person who shows no respect for the thoughts and interests of others is regarded as an abomination by the community.

Verses 10-12 imply that the arrogant in fact shrink back in a time of adversity rather than intervening and rescuing those who are being taken off to death. The dramatic situation evoked here is not specified, but the virtue of standing up to abusive violence is clear and given divine backing. Those who plead ignorance will not deceive the Lord (24:12).

¹⁶Though the just fall seven times,
they rise again,
but the wicked stumble from
only one mishap.
¹⁷Do not rejoice when your enemies
fall,
and when they stumble, do not
let your heart exult,
¹⁸Lest the LORD see it, be displeased
with you,
and withdraw his wrath from
your enemies.

¹⁹Do not be provoked at evildoers,
do not envy the wicked;
²⁰For the evil have no future,
the lamp of the wicked will be
put out.
²¹My son, fear the LORD and the
king;
have nothing to do with those
who hate them;
²²For disaster will issue suddenly,
and calamity from them both,
who knows when?

Verses 13-14 reassert the enduring goodness of wisdom, which, in an appealing metaphor, is like honey to the soul (Ps 19:11). The assurance about the future in verse 14 repeats almost word for word that in 23:18, where it is associated with the temptation to envy sinners.

Verses 15-16 warn against becoming one of the wicked by stalking those who are just. The verb "lie in wait" is the same used of the adulteress in 23:28 (see also 1:18). The just will repeatedly rise again, but the wicked will stumble and fall once and for all (cf. Job 5:17-22).

Yet in verses 17-18 the wise person does not gloat over an enemy's fall (cf. Exod 23:4-5; Lev 19:17-18; Matt 5:22). This kind of exulting is displeasing to the Lord and will cause him to withdraw from enacting justice. In Proverbs 20:22 vengeful intentions presume against the work of divine justice (cf. Rom 12:19).With consciousness of these facets of wisdom in relation to evildoers, the instruction repeats in verses 19-20 the admonition with which it began: do not envy the wicked. Whereas with wisdom one has a future, the wicked have neither (24:14).

What not envying the wicked means, as verse 1 states, is refraining from joining with them or imitating them. The verses between verses 1-2 and 19-20 show how the wise take a different route, one that includes relying on wisdom in all undertakings, avoiding violence, advocating for the abused, and leaving vengeance to God.

"Sayings of the Wise" concludes in verses 21-22 by offering the learner a final summation: "My son, fear the LORD and the king." Reverence of the Lord stands first: obedience to the king, God's guardian of justice and order on earth (21:1) follows. Both Lord and king have the power to bring disasters and calamity on those who set themselves against them and the justice they protect.

V. Further Sayings of the Wise

²³These also are Words of the Wise:
To show partiality in judgment is
not good.
²⁴Whoever says to the guilty party,
"You are innocent,"
will be cursed by nations,
scorned by peoples;
²⁵But those who render just verdicts
will fare well,
and on them will come the
blessing of prosperity.

²⁶An honest reply—
a kiss on the lips.
²⁷Complete your outdoor tasks,
and arrange your work in the
field;
afterward you can build your
house.
²⁸Do not testify falsely against your
neighbor
and so deceive with your lips.
²⁹Do not say, "As they did to me, so
will I do to them;

OTHER SAYINGS OF THE WISE

Proverbs 24:23-34

This small group of sayings is marked as a separate collection by the opening phrase: "These also are Words of the Wise." In its present placement it appears as an appendix to "Sayings of the Wise" (22:17–24:22). It combines short sayings and instructions with slightly longer sequences.

Verse 26 can be seen as part of the discussion of partiality in judgment that precedes it (24:23-25), but it also stands on its own as an example of proverbial wit. The one who returns a straight answer from his or her lips gives a kiss on the lips. Such an answer, in other words, is as delightful as a kiss, and the one who gives it is a true friend.

Verse 27 illustrates the essence of wisdom in a practical context. One's life must be planned out with thought and a long view of the desired outcome. In this case the *means* of living—the field and the work of cultivating it—must be attended to before one builds a house to live in and fills it (the Hebrew word for "house" also means "household"). This instruction serves as an excellent example of the need for deliberation in planning any endeavor, including life itself.

Verse 29 can be read in direct relation to the saying in verse 28 about giving false testimony against a neighbor. It can also be taken more broadly as a warning against retaliation and vengeance, as in 24:17-18.

Verses 30-34 offer a first-person narrative that illustrates the joining of wisdom to perception of life. The speaker passes the untended field of one who is lazy and without sense, observes that it is overgrown with weeds, and reflects on what he has seen (24:30-32). The result is a lesson given not so much in the form of a dictum as of a visual impression of lazy behavior

I will repay them according to
their deeds."
³⁰I passed by the field of a sluggard,
by the vineyard of one with no
sense;
³¹It was all overgrown with thistles;
its surface was covered with
nettles,
and its stone wall broken down.
³²As I gazed at it, I reflected;
I saw and learned a lesson:
³³A little sleep, a little slumber,
a little folding of the arms to
rest—

³⁴Then poverty will come upon you
like a robber,
and want like a brigand.

VI. Second Solomonic Collection, Collected under King Hezekiah

25 ¹These also are proverbs of Solomon. The servants of Hezekiah, king of Judah, transmitted them.
²It is the glory of God to conceal a
matter,
and the glory of kings to fathom
a matter.

("a little sleep, a little slumber, a folding of the arms to rest") and its outcome. Poverty will break into this comfortable oblivion as rudely as a burglar (24:33-34). This micro-narrative, which stresses the integral relation between wisdom and a way of seeing the world, forms a suitable conclusion for the collection of sayings of "the wise" in 22:17–24:34.

OTHER PROVERBS OF SOLOMON

Proverbs 25:1–29:27

These chapters are designated as a distinct collection in 25:1: "These also are proverbs of Solomon. The servants of Hezekiah, king of Judah, transmitted them." This verse, the only reference in Proverbs to the process of composition of the book, is taken by some scholars as a historical colophon, although this cannot be definitively established. Hezekiah, who ruled Judah in the late eighth century B.C., is lauded as a God-fearing and just king in 2 Kings 18–19 and Isaiah 36–37, and the hymn praising an unnamed future king as a "wonderful counselor" in Isaiah 9:1-7 may refer to Hezekiah. His royal legend, then, is similar to Solomon's.

Chapters 25–26 include some thematic sequences of proverbs, and the sayings of chapter 27 conclude with a multi-verse instruction. Chapters 28–29 resume the pattern of antithetically parallel sayings that opens the first collection of Solomon's proverbs. These features suggest some intentional literary shaping.

25:1-28

The series of sayings about the king in verses 2-7 follows naturally the attribution of this collection of proverbs to the servants (probably scribes)

93

³Like the heavens in height, and the earth in depth,
the heart of kings is unfathomable.
⁴Remove the dross from silver,
and it comes forth perfectly purified;
⁵Remove the wicked from the presence of the king,
and his throne is made firm through justice.
⁶Claim no honor in the king's presence,
nor occupy the place of superiors;
⁷For it is better to be told, "Come up closer!"

than to be humbled before the prince.
⁸What your eyes have seen
do not bring forth too quickly against an opponent;
For what will you do later on
when your neighbor puts you to shame?
⁹Argue your own case with your neighbor,
but the secrets of others do not disclose;
¹⁰Lest, hearing it, they reproach you,
and your ill repute never ceases.
¹¹Golden apples in silver settings
are words spoken at the proper time.

of King Hezekiah. In verse 2 the king works in tandem with God, but in a contrasting role. God knows everything, but does not reveal all. It falls to the king to search out and examine what is concealed from ordinary sight. King Solomon does just this in judging the case of the two women who claim the same child (1 Kgs 3:16-28). In verse 3, then, the heart of the king, like that of God, is itself so wide and deep as to be unsearchable (Isa 40:28; Ps 145:3; Job 5:9; 9:10). Clearly the ideal face of kingship is shown here.

The realities of kingship are suggested in the metaphor of verses 4-5. Just as only after dross has been removed from silver is it purified and ready to be shaped into a useful object, so only when wicked hangers-on are purged from the court can the king's throne be firmly founded in justice.

Verses 6-7 speak of the proper attitude toward the king: respect and deference, as opposed to self-promotion and presumption. The "better than" contrast in verse 7 is echoed in the parable in Luke 14:7-11.

Many of the sayings in verses 8-28 heighten sensitivity to the dynamics of personal and social relations: with neighbors (25:8-10, 17, 18), with a ruler (25:15), with enemies (25:21-22), with a spouse (25:24), and with others generally. These verses coach the reader to think about which sorts of actions cause discord with others and which create good will. Among the former are lawsuits (25:8-10), empty promises (25:14), outstaying a welcome (25:7), testifying falsely against a neighbor (25:18), betraying trust (25:19), insensitive levity (25:20), gossip (25:23), argumentativeness (25:24–21:9), and lack of self-control (25:28). Actions and occurrences that build social harmony

¹²A golden earring or a necklace of
  fine gold—
    one who gives wise reproof to a
    listening ear.
¹³Like the coolness of snow in the
  heat of the harvest
    are faithful messengers for those
    who send them,
    lifting the spirits of their mas-
    ters.
¹⁴Clouds and wind but no rain—
    the one who boasts of a gift not
    given.
¹⁵By patience is a ruler persuaded,
    and a soft tongue can break a
    bone.
¹⁶If you find honey, eat only what
  you need,
    lest you have your fill and vomit
    it up.

¹⁷Let your foot be seldom in your
  neighbors' house,
    lest they have their fill of you—
    and hate you.
¹⁸A club, sword, or sharp arrow—
    the one who bears false witness
    against a neighbor.
¹⁹A bad tooth or an unsteady foot—
    a trust betrayed in time of
    trouble.
²⁰Like the removal of clothes on a
  cold day, or vinegar on soda,
    is the one who sings to a
    troubled heart.
²¹If your enemies are hungry, give
  them food to eat,
    if thirsty, give something to
    drink;
²²For live coals you will heap on
    their heads,

---

and well-being include suitable words (25:11), wise correction (25:12), trust-worthy messengers (25:13), patience (literally, "slowness to anger") and a gentle tongue (25:15), and good news from those who are distant (25:25).

Among these sayings are a number of "like" proverbs that make an overt comparison, often between natural and human phenomena. Such compari-sons help define what seem to be puzzling human experiences. In verse 14, for example, the appearance of clouds and wind that never produce rain is compared to one who boasts about a gift that never materializes. Verse 23 also draws on meteorological imagery: the north wind brings rain, and mean gossip, angry faces. On the positive side, a word spoken at just the right time is like something extraordinary: golden apples in silver settings (25:11; cf. 15:23). One who gives wise correction is, similarly, like a golden adornment to a listening ear (25:12; cf. 24:26).

The prescription in verses 21-22 to be generous to one's enemies is con-sistent with the admonitions against vengeance in 20:22 and 24:17-18 (cf. Matt 5:38-42). The metaphor that compares generosity to heaping coals on an adversary's head is taken up by St. Paul in Romans 12:20.

The potential magnitude of the impact of an uncontrolled temper (lit-erally, "spirit") is considered in verse 28. The person without restraint is like a city whose walls have been breached by a hostile invasion. The consequences of military conquest in the ancient world were grim: slavery,

and the Lord will vindicate
  you.
²³The north wind brings rain,
  and a backbiting tongue, angry
    looks.
²⁴It is better to dwell in a corner of
    the housetop
  than in a mansion with a quar-
    relsome wife.
²⁵Cool water to one faint from thirst
  is good news from a far country.
²⁶A trampled fountain or a polluted
    spring—
  a just person fallen before the
    wicked.
²⁷To eat too much honey is not
    good;
  nor to seek honor after honor.
²⁸A city breached and left defenseless

are those who do not control
  their temper.
26 ¹Like snow in summer, like rain
    in harvest,
  honor for a fool is out of place.
²Like the sparrow in its flitting, like
    the swallow in its flight,
  a curse uncalled-for never lands.
³The whip for the horse, the bridle
    for the ass,
  and the rod for the back of fools.
⁴Do not answer fools according to
    their folly,
  lest you too become like them.
⁵Answer fools according to their
    folly,
  lest they become wise in their
    own eyes.
⁶Those who send messages by a
    fool

looting, exile, and death. The language and imagery of this saying make it a mirror opposite of 16:32, in which one who rules over his or her spirit is declared to be better than one who *captures* a city.

26:1-28

Most of the sayings in this chapter concern what it means to be a fool. Some overlap with the sayings of the preceding chapter, since troubling or alienating others is characteristic of fools (11:29; 18:6; 20:3; 22:10). Again, many of these sayings are "like" proverbs that show up the futility of fool-ish behavior or ridicule the fool.

Verse 1 uses a natural image to highlight the inherent incompatibility of honor, or communal acclaim, with the fool. Like snow in summer or rain in harvest, honor for fools is out of the natural order of things. Verse 8 makes the same point but chooses a different analogy, having to do with the misuse of a slingshot.

Verses 4-5 provide a classic example of how even explicit instructions in Proverbs can appear contradictory. On the surface these verses appear to cancel each other out: should one answer fools according to their foolish-ness, or not? These verses could also be seen as balancing or moderating each other. Determining when it is sensible to answer or not to answer, and to what extent, is part of the discipline of discernment.

cut off their feet; they drink
    down violence.
[7]A proverb in the mouth of a fool
    hangs limp, like crippled legs.
[8]Giving honor to a fool
    is like entangling a stone in the
       sling.
[9]A thorn stuck in the hand of a
    drunkard
    is a proverb in the mouth of
       fools.
[10]An archer wounding all who pass
    by
    is anyone who hires a drunken
       fool.
[11]As dogs return to their vomit,
    so fools repeat their folly.
[12]You see those who are wise in
    their own eyes?

There is more hope for fools
    than for them.
[13]The sluggard says, "There is a lion
    in the street,
    a lion in the middle of the
       square!"
[14]The door turns on its hinges
    and sluggards, on their beds.
[15]The sluggard buries a hand in the
    dish,
    too weary to lift it to the mouth.
[16]In their own eyes sluggards are
    wiser
    than seven who answer with
       good judgment.
[17]Whoever meddles in the quarrel
    of another
    is one who grabs a passing dog
       by the ears.

The point of verse 4 is to avoid descending to the level of fools in inter-actions with them: to remain careful and deliberate in one's "answers" or responses. The point of verse 5 is, on the other hand, to assess whom it is you are dealing with and to catch fools up or "answer" them when needed, i.e., "according to their folly." Both the negative ("Answer not") and posi-tive ("Answer") instructions make sense. But both must be undertaken advisedly, with an awareness of the alternative strategy.

Discernment is what the foolish do not undertake, according to the image of verse 7. Even if fools can learn a proverb, it hangs limp or useless in their mouths because they don't know what to do with it (17:16). Verse 9 offers a dif-ferent and more threatening image: a fool wields a proverb the way a drunkard handles a thorn stuck in his hand. The wit of this saying raises the possibility that the thorn represents a barb against fools and foolishness. In verse 10 the harm a fool can do is given further expression in the simile of the employer of a drunken fool, who is compared to an archer recklessly shooting off arrows.

The disinterest of fools in learning is the source of the insult in verse 11, a saying that is well known through its citation in 2 Peter 2:22. The com-parison of a fool to a dog is in itself degrading (see, e.g., 1 Sam 17:43; 2 Sam 3:8, 16:9), even more the elaboration of the dog's behavior. The coupling of a natural canine habit with the reversion of a fool to foolishness implies that the latter is both habitual and instinctive.

¹⁸Like a crazed archer
  scattering firebrands and deadly
    arrows,
¹⁹Such are those who deceive their
    neighbor,
  and then say, "I was only joking."
²⁰Without wood the fire dies out;
  without a talebearer strife sub-
    sides.
²¹Charcoal for coals, wood for fire—
  such are the quarrelsome, en-
    kindling strife.
²²The words of a talebearer are like
  dainty morsels:
  they sink into one's inmost
    being.

²³Like a glazed finish on earthen-
    ware
  are smooth lips and a wicked
    heart.
²⁴With their lips enemies pretend,
  but inwardly they maintain de-
    ceit;
²⁵When they speak graciously, do
    not trust them,
  for seven abominations are in
    their hearts.
²⁶Hatred can be concealed by pre-
    tense,
  but malice will be revealed in
    the assembly.
²⁷Whoever digs a pit falls into it;

Verse 12 measures the fool against what is even worse: one who is wise in his or her own eyes. At the same time the parallelism of the two half-lines encourages us to link the fool with this kind of self-delusion (26:5). Verse 16 asserts that the same defect is endemic to the lazy (26:16), who are vividly ridiculed in verses 13-16 (26:13 repeats 22:13). The comparison in verse 14 is particularly neat. As a door turns on its hinges but goes nowhere, so the lazy person moves in his or her sleep and dreams but does nothing. Within the overall perspective of Proverbs, the lazy embody a particular form of foolishness.

Similarly vivid and recognizable are the portraits of troublemakers in verses 17-19, both the one who interferes in someone else's quarrel and the one who misleads or cheats a neighbor and then tries to laugh it off. Verses 20-26 and 28 speak specifically of the role of negative and deceitful talk in strife and hostility. The sayings in chapter 26 as a whole, then, connect foolishness (26:1-16) with social disturbance (26:17-28), which is a predominant theme in chapter 25.

Verse 27 is often cited as a clear illustration of the wisdom principle of act leading to consequence. The metaphors chosen convey a kind of natural inevitability. The images of a person falling into a pit and a stone rolling back on the one who sets it in motion evoke the law of gravity. In its present placement at the end of chapter 26, this paradigmatic saying can be understood in terms of the negative reaction of the community to fools who disrupt the social order.

and a stone comes back upon
the one who rolls it.
[28]The lying tongue is its owner's
enemy,
and the flattering mouth works
ruin.

27 [1]Do not boast about tomorrow,
for you do not know what
any day may bring forth.
[2]Let another praise you, not your
own mouth;
a stranger, not your own lips.
[3]Stone is heavy, and sand a
burden,
but a fool's provocation is
heavier than both.
[4]Anger is cruel, and wrath over-
whelming,
but before jealousy who can
stand?

[5]Better is an open rebuke
than a love that remains hidden.
[6]Trustworthy are the blows of a
friend,
dangerous, the kisses of an
enemy.
[7]One who is full spurns honey;
but to the hungry, any bitter
thing is sweet.
[8]Like a bird far from the nest
so is anyone far from home.
[9]Perfume and incense bring joy to
the heart,
but by grief the soul is torn
asunder.
[10]Do not give up your own friend
and your father's friend;
do not resort to the house of
your kindred when
trouble strikes.

27:1-27

The sayings in chapter 27 are not grouped thematically, but many of them relate to the theme of social and personal relationships established in chapters 25 and 26. Verse 3 lights on the vexing effect of the fool, which is more burdensome than the weight of stones or sand. Verse 4 differentiates between negative emotions, singling out jealousy as the most difficult to resist (6:34). Verse 5 weighs open rebuke against hidden love. If love keeps thoughts secret, the saying insinuates, it may not be manifesting itself as love in action (24:26). Thus in verse 6 the blows of a friend are accepted as trustworthy.

Verse 10 affirms the value of cultivating supportive relations with friends (literally, "neighbors") and warns against writing them off in times of trouble in favor of distant relatives. Verse 14 offers a very ordinary example of behavior that irritates: a loud greeting to a neighbor early in the morning, no matter what its intention, will be taken as a curse.

Another facet of human interaction is addressed in verse 17. Just as iron striking against iron sharpens it, so one person draws out and sharpens the personhood of another. Verse 19, on the other hand, speaks of the inevitable distance between persons: just as physical appearances (faces) differ, so do internal sensibilities (hearts). Taken together these sayings exhibit the balance between the individual and the interpersonal that is fundamental in Proverbs.

Better a neighbor near than kin far
away.
¹¹Be wise, my son, and bring joy to
my heart,
so that I can answer whoever
taunts me.
¹²The astute see an evil and hide;
the naive continue on and pay
the penalty.
¹³Take the garment of the one who
became surety for a stranger;
if for a foreign woman, exact the
pledge!
¹⁴Those who greet their neighbor
with a loud voice in the early
morning,
a curse can be laid to their
charge.
¹⁵For a persistent leak on a rainy
day
the match is a quarrelsome wife;
¹⁶Whoever would hide her hides a
stormwind
and cannot tell north from
south.
¹⁷Iron is sharpened by iron;
one person sharpens another.

¹⁸Those who tend a fig tree eat its
fruit;
so those attentive to their master
will be honored.
¹⁹As face mirrors face in water,
so the heart reflects the person.
²⁰Sheol and Abaddon can never be
satisfied;
so the eyes of mortals can never
be satisfied.
²¹The crucible for silver, the furnace
for gold,
so you must assay the praise
you receive.
²²Though you pound fools with a
pestle,
their folly never leaves them.
²³Take good care of your flocks,
give careful attention to your
herds;
²⁴For wealth does not last forever,
nor even a crown from age to
age.
²⁵When the grass comes up and the
new growth appears,
and the mountain greens are
gathered in,

Verse 20 compares the insatiability of the underworld for the dead, which is never exhausted, to that of human eyes, which are never satisfied either. The comparison evokes the concept of futility (in 17:24 it is the fool whose eyes are on the ends of the earth). This saying calls to mind the musings of Ecclesiastes on the vanity of human attempts to comprehend the ebb and flow of existence: "The eye is not satisfied by seeing" (Eccl 1:8; 4:8).

Verses 23-27 conclude the chapter with an instruction that speaks of knowledge in relation to the occupation of herding. A literal translation of verse 23 exhorts the listener to "take good care of your flocks" and "give careful attention to your herds." This sort of particular knowledge is placed within the framework of broader knowledge of the cycles and seasons of human and natural life. Wealth, or treasure, does not last forever (27:24). Grass, on the other hand, renews itself and can be gathered and stored to feed one's flocks (27:25). Flocks supply food, clothing, and even the equiva-

²⁶The lambs will provide you with
    clothing,
  and the goats, the price of a
    field,
²⁷And there will be ample goat's
    milk for your food,
  food for your house, sustenance
    for your maidens.

28 ¹The wicked flee though none
    pursue;
  but the just, like a lion, are confi-
    dent.
²If a land is rebellious, its princes
    will be many;
  but with an intelligent and wise
    ruler there is stability.
³One who is poor and extorts from
    the lowly
  is a devastating rain that leaves
    no food.

⁴Those who abandon instruction
    praise the wicked,
  but those who keep instruction
    oppose them.
⁵The evil understand nothing of jus-
    tice,
  but those who seek the Lord
    understand everything.
⁶Better to be poor and walk in in-
    tegrity
  than rich and crooked in one's
    ways.
⁷Whoever heeds instruction is a
    wise son,
  but whoever joins with wastrels
    disgraces his father.
⁸Whoever amasses wealth by inter-
    est and overcharge
  gathers it for the one who is
    kind to the poor.

---

lent of "the price of a field" to support an extended family (27:26-27). The wise farmer will be mindful of these realities and take animal husbandry seriously. This six-verse instruction is reminiscent of the advice on farming and herding that follows the counsels on religious, social, and family life in Hesiod's *Works and Days*. As a culmination of the shorter sayings and instructions in chapters 25–27, it marks the end of a literary section.

28:1-27

Antithetically parallel sayings, many of which display the fundamental divergence between the just and the wicked, predominate in Poverbs 28–29. Since the initial collection of proverbs begins with a similar section of sayings (Prov 10–15), chapters 28–29 form a literary *inclusio* bracketing "The Proverbs of Solomon" (Prov 10:1–22:16) with the "Other Proverbs of Solomon" (Prov 25–29).

Proverbs 28:1 is a prototypical saying that contrasts the fundamental instability of the wicked with the confident security of the just. This contrast is both heightened and made ironic by the comparison of the just person to a lion, a hunting animal. The unscrupulous wicked person, on the other hand, bolts even when no one is in pursuit. The parallelism encourages the reader to envision the wicked as prey.

⁹Those who turn their ears from
hearing instruction,
even their prayer is an abomination.
¹⁰Those who mislead the upright
into an evil way
will themselves fall into their
own pit,
but the blameless will attain
prosperity.
¹¹The rich are wise in their own
eyes,
but the poor who are intelligent
see through them.
¹²When the just triumph, there is
great glory;
but when the wicked prevail,
people hide.
¹³Those who conceal their sins do
not prosper,
but those who confess and forsake them obtain mercy.
¹⁴Happy those who always fear;
but those who harden their
hearts fall into evil.
¹⁵A roaring lion or a ravenous bear
is a wicked ruler over a poor
people.

¹⁶The less prudent the rulers, the
more oppressive their deeds.
Those who hate ill-gotten gain
prolong their days.
¹⁷Though a person burdened with
blood guilt is in flight even
to the grave,
let no one offer support.
¹⁸Whoever walks blamelessly is safe,
but one whose ways are crooked
falls into a pit.
¹⁹Those who cultivate their land
will have plenty of food,
but those who engage in idle
pursuits will have plenty
of want.
²⁰The trustworthy will be richly
blessed;
but whoever hastens to be rich
will not go unpunished.
²¹To show partiality is never good:
for even a morsel of bread one
may do wrong.
²²Misers hurry toward wealth,
not knowing that want is coming toward them.
²³Whoever rebukes another wins
more favor

Verses 4-5 illustrate the inherent clash of perspectives between the just and the wicked. In verse 4 the point of view is defined by instruction, which refers to the traditional teaching of the community (cf. 28:7). Those who abandon this teaching praise the wicked; those who hold onto it clash with wrongdoers (29:10, 27). The image of pitched conflict and the plural forms ("those who . . .") create an impression of social division.

Verse 5 presents a similar opposition. The wicked cannot understand what justice is. Those who seek the Lord, on the other hand, understand it fully. The Lord is the source of justice (Pss 50, 94, 96–97, 99), so those who seek to know God come to understand it. The sights of the wicked are fixed elsewhere, and justice does not enter their view (21:15; 29:7, 10). Wisdom 2–5 features a similar disjunction between the perception of the wicked and that of the just.

"A roaring lion . . . is a wicked ruler over a poor people" (Prov 28:15).

than one who flatters with the
tongue.
²⁴Whoever defrauds father or mother
and says, "It is no sin,"
is a partner to a brigand.
²⁵The greedy person stirs up strife,
but the one who trusts in the
Lord will prosper.
²⁶Those who trust in themselves are
fools,
but those who walk in wisdom
are safe.
²⁷Those who give to the poor have
no lack,

but those who avert their eyes,
many curses.
²⁸When the wicked prevail, people
hide;
but at their fall the just
abound.

29 ¹Those stiff-necked in the face of
reproof
in an instant will be shattered
beyond cure.
²When the just flourish, the people
rejoice;
but when the wicked rule, the
people groan.

Verse 13 steps beyond the stark contrast between just and wicked to speak of the reality of human transgression. Those who hope to get ahead by concealing their misdeeds won't, but those who openly admit and abandon their wrongdoing can expect mercy.

Verse 28 considers the wider social dynamics of the just and the wicked. The dominance of the wicked in a community establishes a climate of fear, sending people into hiding (28:15; Amos 5:13). Conversely, when the wicked vanish the just can multiply and thrive (cf. 28:12; 29:2, 16). In 29:16, crime increases when the wicked are many.

29:1-27

A number of sayings in this chapter continue the theme of the societal and political impact of the just and the wicked, the foolish and the wise. Several reflect on the character of the king or ruler. In verse 4 the king who brings stability to a land through justice is contrasted with the one who by overtaxing destroys its prosperity. Taxes, tithes, and voluntary contributions are not by definition unjust in the Old Testament (see, e.g., Deut 12:6, where they support the temple), but Deuteronomy 17:14-20 warns against excessive royal expenditures. Further, the account of Solomon in 1 Kings 4–12 links his taxation and forced labor policies with the eventual breakup of his kingdom. Verse 12 observes that if a ruler pays attention to false talk (including perhaps flattery), all who work for him will be wicked.

Verse 8 sets a contrast between the arrogant and the wise in terms of their impact on the social body. The arrogant inflame a city, presumably because they take counsel with no one and hold others in contempt. The wise in contrast are able to negotiate and to turn back the course of anger.

³Whoever loves wisdom gives joy
to his father,
but whoever consorts with har-
lots squanders his wealth.
⁴By justice a king builds up the land;
but one who raises taxes tears it
down.
⁵Those who speak flattery to their
neighbor
cast a net at their feet.
⁶The sin of the wicked is a trap,
but the just run along joyfully.
⁷The just care for the cause of the
poor;
the wicked do not understand
such care.

⁸Scoffers enflame the city,
but the wise calm the fury.
⁹If a wise person disputes with a
fool,
there is railing and ridicule but
no resolution.
¹⁰The bloodthirsty hate the blameless,
but the upright seek his life.
¹¹Fools give vent to all their anger;
but the wise, biding their time,
control it.
¹²If rulers listen to lying words,
their servants all become
wicked.
¹³The poor and the oppressor meet:

Verse 13 points out a mystery of the social body, in which poor and oppressor coexist in the same community. The saying observes only that the Lord gives light to the eyes of both (cf. 22:2). Read from one perspective, it points to divine tolerance of both oppressed and oppressor, and seems to counter the assertion in 13:9 that "the light of the just gives joy, but the lamp of the wicked goes out" (cf. 24:20). In this it echoes reflections on God's justice in wisdom writings like Job (Job 21:17; 24:21-23; but see 38:15), Ecclesiastes (Eccl 4:1-3; 7:15-18), and Sirach (Sir 33:10-15). Read from another perspective, it asserts that the poor are no less important to God than the powerful (Job 31:13-15; Sir 11:1-6).

The role of vision in the social body is the subject of verse 18. Vision in the Old Testament refers to divine communication, almost always in the context of prophecy. Without such communications from God, a people is unrestrained because they lack divine guidance (Amos 8:11-12). The second half-line of the verse contrasts with the first but makes a slightly different claim: the one who follows instruction is happy. Again, the full saying opens up many avenues of meaning. The antithetic parallelism implies: (1) that an unrestrained people is not happy, (2) that the imparting of divine vision enables the observance of traditional teaching (see the connection of *torah*, or priestly instruction, and prophetic vision in Lam 2:9), and (3) that even though the people as a whole abandon restraint, some members of the community may still respect the tradition by their actions. Altogether this proverb provides a glimpse of the interface of prophecy and the teaching of the wise (cf. Ezek 7:26).

the LORD gives light to the eyes
of both.
[14]If a king is honestly for the rights
of the poor,
his throne stands firm forever.
[15]The rod of correction gives wisdom,
but uncontrolled youths disgrace their mothers.
[16]When the wicked increase, crime
increases;
but the just will behold their
downfall.
[17]Discipline your children, and they
will bring you comfort,
and give delight to your soul.
[18]Without a vision the people lose
restraint;
but happy is the one who follows instruction.
[19]Not by words alone can servants
be trained;
for they understand but do not
respond.
[20]Do you see someone hasty in
speech?

There is more hope for a fool!
[21]If servants are pampered from
childhood
they will turn out to be stubborn.
[22]The ill-tempered stir up strife,
and the hotheaded cause many
sins.
[23]Haughtiness brings humiliation,
but the humble of spirit acquire
honor.
[24]Partners of a thief hate themselves;
they hear the imprecation but
do not testify.
[25]Fear of others becomes a snare,
but the one who trusts in the
LORD is safe.
[26]Many curry favor with a ruler,
but it is from the LORD that one
receives justice.
[27]An abomination to the just, the
evildoer;
an abomination to the wicked,
one whose way is
straight.

Verse 26 reminds readers of the ultimate justice of the Lord, to which even the greatest holders of human power are subject. Those who seek a favorable hearing from a ruler might do best first to seek favor with God. Moreover, those who are eager to win favor from a ruler will not escape God's dispensation of justice.

The fundamental incompatibility of the upright and the unjust is pitched in strong language and with exact antithetic parallelism in verse 27. The two modes of being are mutually incomprehensible (29:27). The word "abomination" is used here to convey the mutually exclusive limits that define the perspectives and practices of the wicked and the just. This verse provides a suitable closing for chapters 28–29, which begin in 28:1 with a similar opposition. In the context of the proverbs of Solomon as a whole, it can be read as delineating with final clarity the choice between ways of life that is a constant theme in the sayings. This closing verse implies that the choice is both necessary because the ways do not coincide, and profound because each entails a world view.

VII. Sayings of Agur and Others

30 ¹The words of Agur, son of Jakeh the Massaite:

The pronouncement of mortal man:
"I am weary, O God;
I am weary, O God, and I am exhausted.
²I am more brute than human being,
without even human intelligence;
³Neither have I learned wisdom,
nor have I the knowledge of the Holy One.
⁴Who has gone up to heaven and come down again—
who has cupped the wind in the hollow of the hand?
Who has bound up the waters in a cloak—
who has established all the ends of the earth?
What is that person's name, or the name of his son?"

THE WORDS OF AGUR

Proverbs 30:1-33

This chapter represents a further collection of sayings, attributed in verse 1 to Agur, son of Jakeh the Massaite. The collection is uniquely designated as a pronouncement or oracle and its tone and form are distinct from the collections of sayings that precede it. It begins with Agur's meditation on the limitations of human knowledge in light of the limitlessness and reliability of divine wisdom (30:1-6). This is followed by his prayer for an appropriate posture toward the Lord (30:7-9), a list of arrogant behaviors and attitudes (30:11-14), and a series of numerical sayings (cf. 6:6-19) that reveal the patterns of creation (30:15-31; cf. 6:16-19). Short instructions or sayings punctuate the chapter in verses 10, 17, 24, and 32-33. The words of Agur then break with the standard variation between short sayings and instructions, introducing new literary forms. In this respect the chapter resembles wisdom writings like Job, Ecclesiastes, and Sirach.

The identification of Agur as a Massaite in verse 1 makes him a member of one of the northern Arabian tribes. The tradition of legendary wisdom among the peoples to the east of Israel appears also in the book of Job, where Job and at least some of his friends are Edomites (Job 1:1; 2:11), and in the book of Obadiah, which refers to the wisdom of Edom (see Obad 8). The inclusion of a voice from outside Israel indicates the universal reach of wisdom.

The term *oracle* is used most often of divine revelation in prophetic contexts (e.g., Num 23:7, 18; 24:1-4, 15-16). Agur speaks for himself in the first person, yet his oracle draws attention to the "word of God" (30:5). Somewhat surprisingly, at the end of Proverbs this teacher of wisdom delivers an oracle that denies any claim to human wisdom.

⁵Every word of God is tested;
  he is a shield to those who take
    refuge in him.
⁶Add nothing to his words,
  lest he reprimand you, and you
    be proved a liar.

⁷Two things I ask of you,
  do not deny them to me before I
    die:
⁸Put falsehood and lying far from me,
  give me neither poverty nor
    riches;

provide me only with the food I
  need;
⁹Lest, being full, I deny you,
  saying, "Who is the LORD?"
Or, being in want, I steal,
  and profane the name of my God.
¹⁰Do not criticize servants to their
    master,
  lest they curse you, and you
    have to pay the penalty.
¹¹There are some who curse their fa-
    thers,
  and do not bless their mothers.

Agur begins in verses 1-6 with a lament over the finitude of his own wisdom: "Neither have I learned wisdom, / nor have I the knowledge of the Holy One" (30:3). The series of rhetorical questions in verse 4 evoke a sense of the immeasurable knowledge of God and resemble those posed by God to Job in Job 38–39 (cf. Isa 40:12-17). The lament ends in verses 5-6 with an affirmation that God's words prove true against all challenges and that they should form the foundation and end of human knowledge ("Add nothing to his words"). By the word of God Agur means the law and prophetic revelation (cf. Deut 4:2). Agur's wisdom can only recognize the incomparability of divine wisdom and take refuge in it (30:5). All else is deceptive, and those who know this find true protection from life's ills.

The prayer of Agur in verses 7-9 reflects his orientation toward divine wisdom. As a teacher of wisdom, Agur asks God to keep him away from what is false (30:6). This request is coupled with his plea to be given neither poverty nor wealth, for either state might distance him from God. Agur asks, in effect, that he always be conscious of his dependence on the providence of the Lord. These verses are the only instance of a prayer in Proverbs.

Verses 11-14 list four categories of people, each of which can be seen as rejecting divine wisdom. The first group, who curse their parents (30:1), and the last group, who exploit the poor and weak (30:14), exhibit behavior that strikes at the heart of the ethical tradition of Israel (see Exod 20:12; 22:24-26). They frame two groups who are faulted for their attitudes: self-delusion (30:12) and pride (30:13).

Verses 15-33 contain a series of five longer sayings interspersed with shorter proverbs. The former are known as "numerical proverbs" because they take the form of a listing of diverse objects and phenomena. A characteristic numbering formula gives the number of things listed in a two-part

¹²There are some pure in their own
  eyes,
    yet not cleansed of their filth.
¹³There are some—how haughty
  their eyes!
    how overbearing their glance!
¹⁴There are some—their teeth are
  swords,
    their teeth are knives,
Devouring the needy from the earth,
  and the poor from the human
    race.
¹⁵The leech has two daughters:
  "Give," and "Give."
Three things never get their fill,
  four never say, "Enough!"
¹⁶Sheol, a barren womb,
  land that never gets its fill of
    water,

and fire, which never says,
  "Enough!"
¹⁷The eye that mocks a father,
  or scorns the homage due a
    mother,
Will be plucked out by brook ravens;
  devoured by a brood of vul-
    tures.
¹⁸Three things are too wonderful for
  me,
    yes, four I cannot understand:
¹⁹The way of an eagle in the sky,
  the way of a serpent upon a
    rock,
The way of a ship on the high seas,
  and the way of a man with a
    woman.
²⁰This is the way of an adulterous
  woman:

sequence: for example, in verse 18: "Three things are . . yes, four. . . " (cf. 6:16-19). The common thread running through each list is stated in the opening lines. Yet the sayings retain a riddle-like quality in that the reader is left to ponder exactly how the phenomena named manifest the common feature and relate to each other. By joining unlikely phenomena these sayings of Agur convey a sense of the enigmatic patterning of creation that echoes his affirmation of the transcendence of divine wisdom.

Of the five numerical sayings, three join human and natural phenomena (30:15-17, 18-20, and 29-31), one names only human figures (30:21-23), and one only animals (30:24-28). The overall mix evokes the totality of creation in its various aspects.

The numerical sayings thus continue the theme of reverence for divine wisdom raised in verses 3-6. At the same time they encourage the student of wisdom to contemplate the face of creation. The interspersing of more typical proverbs among the numerical sayings in verses 17, 20, and 32-33 suggests that these riddles of the natural and human worlds are to be seen as an integral element in the acquisition of wisdom (6:6-8; cf. 1 Kgs 5:12-14).

The first saying (30:15-16) does not begin with the characteristic numerical formula but with an arresting image (the leech and his daughters) that signals the theme of the saying, which is insatiability. Four things are never satisfied: the underworld, or realm of the dead (27:20); a womb that cannot

she eats, wipes her mouth,
and says, "I have done no
wrong."
²¹Under three things the earth
trembles,
yes, under four it cannot bear up:
²²Under a slave who becomes king,
and a fool who is glutted with
food;
²³Under an unloved woman who is
wed,
and a maidservant who dis-
places her mistress.

²⁴Four things are among the small-
est on the earth,
and yet are exceedingly wise:
²⁵Ants—a species not strong,
yet they store up their food in
the summer;
²⁶Badgers—a species not mighty,
yet they make their home in the
crags;
²⁷Locusts—they have no king,
yet they march forth in formation;
²⁸Lizards—you can catch them with
your hands,

---

conceive; the dry earth; and fire. The first and last in this list concern death and destruction, which exert a continuous pull on life, and the middle two, the drive toward regeneration of life, which pushes forward simultaneously.

The saying in verses 18-19 is probably the best known, and its theme is wonder. The mystery of traversing the realms of sky, earth, and sea form a cosmic background for the climactic journey: the way of a man with a young woman. That this is the most wondrous phenomenon of all is implicit in its final position and in its contrast to what precedes. The flight of an eagle, the passage of a snake, and the course of a ship leave no trace, but the life of a man and woman together has the potential of generating new life.

In verses 21-23 what seems to hold the four situations named together is the anticipation of excessive behavior. This saying points to the granting of power (to the slave and the maidservant), position (to the hated woman), and satisfaction (to the fool) to persons who will probably not handle these states well (19:10; 26:1). The pattern of overcompensation for past deprivation is evoked in the cases of the slave, the maidservant, and the woman, and the fool is drawn into this pattern as well. Foolish behavior typically results in failure and shame, but the fool whose needs are satisfied may gain new confidence in his or her approach to life and act all the more foolishly.

Verses 24-28 trace a pattern in the animal world. As in 6:6-8, where the lazy son is urged to observe the ways of the ant, the reader is given examples in the form of various small creatures, including the ant. The point is that wisdom is more important than power and strength (24:5). With wisdom, ants think ahead to gather in summer their food for the winter, badgers are able to construct their houses in rocky cliffs, locusts move together in synchrony, and lizards small enough to be held in the hand reside in king's

yet they find their way into
kings' palaces.
²⁹Three things are stately in their
stride,
yes, four are stately in their car-
riage:
³⁰The lion, mightiest of beasts,
retreats before nothing;
³¹The strutting cock, and the he-
goat,
and the king at the head of his
people.
³²If you have foolishly been proud
or presumptuous—put your
hand on your mouth;

³³For as the churning of milk produces curds,
and the pressing of the nose
produces blood,
the churning of anger produces
strife.

VIII. Sayings of King Lemuel

31 ¹The words of Lemuel, king of
Massa, the instruction his
mother taught him:

²What are you doing, my son!
what are you doing, son of my
womb;

palaces. The lack of a human example in the list calls recalls Agur's question about what human wisdom amounts to (30:2-3). This numerical saying
bears out the common assertion that biblical wisdom has to do with the
contemplation of creation in all its aspects, though always with reference
to enlightening human ways (cf., e.g., Job 38–39).

The mix of animals and a human king in verses 29-31 has, in one sense,
a leveling effect. The common thread in this saying is the emergence of
leaders in diverse species: the lion, the rooster, and the he-goat all have
distinctive gaits that place them in front of those they lead, and so does a
king. On the one hand, placing human kingship within the natural order of
things demystifies royalty. The king's responsibility appears here in a different light than it does in the psalms that praise him as divinely anointed
and a son of God (Ps 2, 45). At the same time, kingship is shown to be an
inherent part of the creative design.

THE WORDS OF LEMUEL

Proverbs 31:1-31

The final chapter of Proverbs is presented as the words of a mother to
her royal son, thus balancing the speeches of the father to his son in the
introduction to the book (Prov 1–9). King Lemuel, like Agur, is a Massaite
(31:1). He is also a king, a sign of the royal as well as the universal aspect of
wisdom. As in 8:15-17, royal attributes of judgment and comportment are
extended by implication to all (Wis 1:1; 6). Verses 1-9 are in the form of an
instruction, a series of positive and negative guidelines. Verses 10-31 form

what are you doing, son of my
vows!
³Do not give your vigor to women,
or your strength to those who
ruin kings.
⁴It is not for kings, Lemuel,
not for kings to drink wine;
strong drink is not for princes,
⁵Lest in drinking they forget what
has been decreed,
and violate the rights of any
who are in need.

⁶Give strong drink to anyone who
is perishing,
and wine to the embittered;
⁷When they drink, they will forget
their misery,
and think no more of their
troubles.
⁸Open your mouth in behalf of the
mute,
and for the rights of the destitute;
⁹Open your mouth, judge justly,
defend the needy and the poor!

---

a separate section as a poem or ode extolling the woman who embodies
the virtues of wisdom.

31:1-9

This closing instruction echoes the claim of personified wisdom in 8:15:
"By me kings reign." The voice of wisdom is heard in the words of the king's
mother. A personal and serious tone is set by the repetition of phrases at the
beginning and end of the instruction (31:2, 4, and 8-9), especially in verse
2: "What are you doing, my son! / what are you doing, son of my womb;
/ what are you doing, son of my vows!" The phrase "Son of my womb"
conveys the tenderness of the mother's pleading; the phrase "son of my
vows" expresses gravity. The "vow" probably refers to a vow made by the
mother to God in hopes of receiving a son, like Hannah's vow in 1 Sam 1:11.
Such a vow might involve, as in the story of Hannah, a pledge to raise the
child in a special relationship to God (see also the nazirite vow in the account of Samson's birth in Judg 13:3-7, 12-14). The vow of Lemuel's mother
would have been answered by the birth of a future king, who would grow
up to bear unique responsibilities. These are what the mother reminds her
son of in what follows, as the twofold repetition of the phrase "it is not for
kings, Lemuel" in verse 4 underscores.

The king's mother steers him away from excesses that could erode his
royal role. Verse 3 concerns sexual relations and the diversion of the king's
energies to them. The account of Solomon's relations with his many foreign
wives in 1 Kings 11:1-13 illustrates this possibility (cf. Deut 17:17). In verses
4-7 the mother warns against the overuse of wine, a symbol of festivity that
is carried too far (Amos 6:4-8; Isa 5:11-13; 28:1). Such overconsumption can
lead a ruler both to forget his responsibility for upholding the laws of the
land and to violate the rights of the powerless (31:5). Drink as a medium of

IX. Poem on the Woman of Worth

10Who can find a woman of worth?
Far beyond jewels is her value.
11Her husband trusts her judgment;
he does not lack income.
12She brings him profit, not loss,
all the days of her life.
13She seeks out wool and flax
and weaves with skillful hands.
14Like a merchant fleet,
she secures her provisions from
afar.

15She rises while it is still night,
and distributes food to her
household,
a portion to her maidservants.
16She picks out a field and acquires
it;
from her earnings she plants a
vineyard.
17She girds herself with strength;
she exerts her arms with vigor.
18She enjoys the profit from her
dealings;

---

escape is appropriate for those who live in misery and despair (31:6-7), but the king's mandate is different. It is spelled out in verses 8-9 with the repetition of the positive imperative, "Open your mouth." The king must speak out for the voiceless and destitute and by doing so, rule justly (29:4, 14).

Placed at the end of an anthology of diverse wisdom writings, this royal instruction is clearly intended for a wider audience. It can be read with broad implications for self-control, sobriety, and a fundamental commitment to upholding justice and advocating for the weak. The royal framework lends climactic significance to this final instruction, reminding the reader of the social as well as personal ramifications of wisdom.

31:10-31 The Woman of Worth

These verses form an acrostic poem, one in which each line or section begins with a successive letter of the Hebrew alphabet (see, e.g., Pss 119, 145). This poetic device is used here for a concluding poem that presents a summation of wisdom from, as it were, *a* to *z*.

The poem to the woman of worth parallels the poems praising wisdom in chapters 1–9, especially those in which wisdom is personified as a woman. In 31:10-31, however, wisdom takes the shape of a real woman in her daily activities. This is the companion to whom a young man should pledge himself, and this the life he can hope to share with her. She is essentially worthy (literally, strong) in her character and her actions. The larger than life depiction of her conveys this strength: she is outstanding in all she says, does, and feels (31:29).

The poem begins with three verses that express the value of the worthy woman in language that parallels the praise of wisdom in chapters 1–9. The question, "Who can find a woman of worth?" recalls the language of seeking and finding wisdom in the wisdom poems (3:13; 8:17, 35). Such a woman is

her lamp is never extinguished at night.
[19]She puts her hands to the distaff, and her fingers ply the spindle.
[20]She reaches out her hands to the poor, and extends her arms to the needy.
[21]She is not concerned for her household when it snows— all her charges are doubly clothed.
[22]She makes her own coverlets;

fine linen and purple are her clothing.
[23]Her husband is prominent at the city gates as he sits with the elders of the land.
[24]She makes garments and sells them, and stocks the merchants with belts.
[25]She is clothed with strength and dignity, and laughs at the days to come.

to be valued beyond jewels (3:15; 8:11). She has, above all, judgment (literally, heart, the faculty of discernment) and will bring her husband abundance and good things as long as she lives (3:16-18; 8:5, 18-21). That a wife could do otherwise is implied in the qualification "good, and not evil" in verse 12.

Verses 13-24 are a portrait in motion of this woman. Her wisdom is manifest in what she does. As a doer she works with willing hands the wool and flax she gathers (31:13). The ambit of her efforts, like that of merchant ships, reaches far away (31:14), yet she does not neglect her household, rising early each day to make sure all within it are fed (31:15). The motif of active hands continues in verses 16-17, 19-20 and in verse 31, where "the work of her hands" is acclaimed.

Verses 21-22 and 24 highlight examples of her handiwork. Spinning and weaving were considered feminine arts throughout the ancient world. In the *Odyssey*, for example, Penelope, the wise counterpart to her shrewd husband Odysseus, spends her days weaving. One can compare the reference to the women skilled (literally, "wise") at spinning in Exodus 35:25-26.

The activities of the worthy woman are not limited to cloth-making, however. She is productive in many ways, for whatever she does yields positive results. She deliberates over a field, decides to buy it, and investing what she has already earned from her handiwork, plants a vineyard (31:16). She shows her generosity by reaching her hands to the poor (31:20). Her helpful influence on her spouse is evident by the recognition and respect shown him at the city gate (31:23; cf. 24:7). What this woman does is known not just by her household but in the community at large.

All these activities build up a character that is described in verses 25-29. In an apt word play, the worthy woman is "clothed" with strength and

²⁶She opens her mouth in
wisdom;
kindly instruction is on her
tongue.
²⁷She watches over the affairs of her
household,
and does not eat the bread of
idleness.
²⁸Her children rise up and call her
blessed;
her husband, too, praises her:

²⁹"Many are the women of proven
worth,
but you have excelled them all."
³⁰Charm is deceptive and beauty
fleeting;
the woman who fears the LORD
is to be praised.
³¹Acclaim her for the work of her
hands,
and let her deeds praise her at
the city gates.

dignity (31:25a). This clothing, too, she has made with her hands: with what she has done and the way she has lived. These qualities protect and enhance her like clothing, enabling her to face the future with hope: "[she] laughs at the days to come" (31:25b), just as wisdom herself plays or laughs before the Lord and over the entire earth (8:30-31).

The strength of character she possesses strengthens others as well. The woman of worth shares her wisdom, imparting kind advice: literally "the teaching (*torah*) of kindness is on her tongue" (31:26). As does the teaching of the mother in the parental instructions (1:8 and 6:20), her words form others in the essential values of wisdom. She protectively watches over the activities of those in her care and does so tirelessly (31:27; cf. 15:3).

For these reasons, those who know her best acclaim her worth. Her children call her blessed or happy, and her husband prizes her above all others (31:28-29; cf. 12:4).

Verses 30-31 offer a final summation, bringing praise of this woman's many strengths into alignment with the reverence toward God that is the beginning of wisdom (1:7). Charm can be deceptive and beauty fleeting, but what endures as praiseworthy over the long term is a woman who fears the Lord (31:30). Such a woman will experience herself the fruit of what her hands have nurtured, and all she has done will sing her praises well beyond her immediate circle in the public arena of the city gates (31:31).

The pairing of father's and mother's instruction and the invitation of woman wisdom to companionship in the introduction to Proverbs is thus matched at the end of the book by the marriage of the discerning man with the woman of strength. In this final poem, the promises of personified wisdom with which the book begins are realized in the union with a human woman who creates a life in accord with her reverence of the Lord.

REVIEW AIDS AND DISCUSSION TOPICS

Introduction to the Book of Proverbs *(pages 5–13)*

1. What is the relationship of the traditional ethos reflected in Proverbs to the ethos reflected in the biblical law codes and prophetic literature?

2. What are the origins of the varied material in Proverbs? Who was responsible for composing and compiling the book in its present form? During what periods did the composition of the book occur?

3. What major literary forms are used in Proverbs, and how do they communicate?

4. How do the sayings, in particular, teach wisdom? What is their impact on the reader?

5. What is the nature of wisdom in Proverbs, and what does the process of acquiring it involve?

6. Who is the "wise" person in Proverbs? Who is the "fool"?

7. What are the limits of wisdom in this book?

8. What challenges does Proverbs pose from the perspective of gender? How can one work with these challenges when reading the book?

1:1–9:18 The Introduction to Proverbs *(pages 15–44)*

1. What are the dimensions of wisdom in 1:1-7?

2. How does the parallelism in 1:7 inform your understanding of the fear of the Lord as the beginning of knowledge?

3. How do the parental speeches and the wisdom poems in 1:8–9:18 complement each other?

4. How is the process of gaining wisdom outlined in Proverbs 2?

5. How is the metaphor of wisdom as a way or path in life developed in the introduction? Which passages in particular use this metaphor?

6. Why is adultery emphasized so much in the parental speeches? How is it a paradigmatic form of foolishness? What approaches does the father take to discourage his son from adultery?

7. What is the effect on the reader of the personification of wisdom in 1:20-33; 3:16-17; 8:1-36; and 9:1-6?

8. What is wisdom's role in creation in 3:19-20? In 8:22-31?

9. How does the introduction to Proverbs end in Proverbs 9, and how does it prepare the reader for the body of the book?

10:1–22:16 The Proverbs of Solomon *(pages 45–82)*

1. What areas of life do these proverbs touch on?

2. What recurrent sets of oppositions appear in chapters 10–15?

3. How is a relationship between act and consequence spelled out in these sayings?

4. Are there pairs or groups of proverbs that seem to contradict each other? How can one best approach these contradictions?

5. What is the relationship between those sayings that mention the role of the Lord in human life and the many more that do not?

6. How do the sayings in 14:12; 16:1-3, 9, 25; 19:21; 20:9, 24 alter the overall tenor of the sayings?

7. How would you characterize the teaching mode(s) of these sayings?

22:17–24:34 Sayings of the Wise and Other Sayings of the Wise *(pages 83–93)*

1. What differences in literary form distinguish "Sayings of the Wise" (22:17–24:22) from "The Proverbs of Solomon" (10:1–22:16)?

2. To what particular audience might 22:22–23:11 be addressed?

3. What do the sayings in 24:1-22 advise on the question of one's relation to evildoers?

4. How does the sketch in 24:28-34 serve as a paradigm of the relation of wisdom to the way one views life?

25:1–29:27 Other Proverbs of Solomon *(pages 93–106)*

1. What does the attribution of this collection to the "men of Hezekiah" (25:1) imply?

2. What sorts of phenomena are compared in the "like" sayings in 25–26? How are these comparisons effective?

3. How do the sayings in chapters 25–27 draw attention to the realities of social interaction?

4. What is the significance of the advice on herding in 27:23-27?

5. What is the interplay between the individual and social aspects of the just and the wicked in chapters 28–29?

6. How is the theme of the incompatibility of the just and the wicked developed in chapters 28–29?

30:1–31:31 The Words of Agur and The Words of Lemuel *(pages 107–15)*

1. What is surprising about the lament of Agur in 30:1-6? How does he limit the pursuit of wisdom?

2. What is the significance of Agur's two requests of God in 30:7-9? How do they relate to his lament over his ignorance in 30:1-4?

3. Compare the way the numerical sayings (30:15-16, 18-19, 21-23, 24-28, and 29-31) and the shorter sayings in other chapters use comparisons to heighten awareness.

4. What meanings do you draw from each of the five numerical sayings?

5. What impression of kingship is given in 31:1-9? How is this teaching, addressed to a king, to be received by a non-royal audience?

6. In what ways do the words of Lemuel's mother serve as a suitable closing instruction, balancing the parental speeches in the introduction to Proverbs?

7. What are the characteristics of the worthy woman in 31:10-31? What overall impression does she make?

8. How do her qualities reflect wisdom? How is the worth of this woman to be compared with wisdom's worth?

9. How is this poem a fitting conclusion to the book of Proverbs?

INDEX OF CITATIONS FROM THE
CATECHISM OF THE CATHOLIC CHURCH

The arabic number(s) following the citation refer(s) to the paragraph number(s) in the *Catechism of the Catholic Church*. The asterisk following a paragraph number indicates that the citation has been paraphrased.

Proverbs

1:8	2214*	17:6	2219
6:20-22	2216	18:5	2476*
8:1–9:6	721*	19:9	2476*
8:7	2465*	19:21	303
8:22-31	288*	21:1	269*
13:1	2216	25:9-10	2489*
14:15	1806		